FROM LOTHIAN

Edited by Dave Thomas

First published in Great Britain in 2000 by
YOUNG WRITERS
Remus House,
Coltsfoot Drive,
Woodston,
Peterborough, PE2 9JX
Telephone (01733) 890066

HB ISBN 0 75431 914 8
SB ISBN 0 75431 915 6

FOREWORD

This year, the Young Writers' Future Voices competition proudly presents a showcase of the best poetic talent from over 42,000 up-and-coming writers nationwide.

Successful in continuing our aim of promoting writing and creativity in children, our regional anthologies give a vivid insight into the thoughts, emotions and experiences of today's younger generation, displaying their inventive writing in its originality.

The thought, effort, imagination and hard work put into each poem impressed us all and again the task of editing proved challenging due to the quality of entries received, but was nevertheless enjoyable. We hope you are as pleased as we are with the final selection and that you continue to enjoy *Future Voices From Lothian* for many years to come.

CONTENTS

Thomas A Hutson	68
Sophie McCabe	68
Kezia Lewis	69
Adam Perry	70
Duncan Fraser	70

Kingsinch School

Steven Donoghue	71

Portobello High School

Laura Fraser	71
Sarah Kwan	72
Natalie O'Loan	73
Gillian Vesco	74
Samantha Brockie	75
Alison Freeman	76
Stacey Lee Drew	76

St David's High School, Dalkeith

Lauren Banks	77
Laura Herriot	77
Carrie Cunningham	78
Scott Galbraith	78
Suzanne Rankin	79
Donna Edie	79
Laura Gillies	80
Lisa Hume	80
Sarah Grealis	81
Andrew Nicolson	81
Jennifer Griffin	82
Lee McNeish	82
Ashley McFarnon	83
Gary Miller	83
Nicola Niven	84
Vikki Hamilton	84
Fergus McGlone	85
Eamonn Reynolds	85
Steven Rose	86

Ian McManus	86
Nicola Rowan	87
Gary Dickson	87
Sara Toule	88
Lyndsay Wyse	89
Lee-Anne Partenheimer	89
Keith Barr	90
Andrew Clarke	91
Ruth Clarke	92
Matthew Coyle	93
Tracey Moffat	93
Marc Dickson	94
Paul Fitzsimmons	94
Matthew Glynn	95
David Thomas	96
Rosina Marr	96
Emma Rattray	97
Lyndsay Paterek	97
Russell Kyle	98
Katie Main	98
Lauren Arthur	99
Heather Stafford	100
Linda Korotkich	100
Steven Nethery	101
Jacqueline Wilson	102
Ruaraidh Szanel	102
Naomi Cameron	103
Craig Glen	104
Lindsey Traynor	104
Steven Colston	105
Alan Meikle	106
Craig McKenzie	106
Louise Severn	107

St Margaret's & St Denis & Cranley School
Shereen Peshrowian	108

Trinity Academy

Whitburn Academy

The Poems

SPACEMAN

If I were a spaceman with a bubble head, I'd zap aliens
then go to bed.

I'd visit all the planets looking for a pal, not small but
thin, green and very, very tall.

We'd play at Star Wars, Star Trek, football or chess for
in the stratosphere we'd be the best.

I'd take him home to Mum and have our tea, sputnik pie,
galaxy burgers and for pud a Milky Way.

I'd ask Mum if he could stay the night for we'd go to bed
all snug and tight but not to let the bedbugs bite.

Steven Scott (11)
Barnardo's Blackford Brae Project

SOUNDS

I love noise
I like:
The sound of rain rattling on the roof,
The sound of feet thumping along the road,
The sound of a roaring car,
The sound of the crash of thunder,
The sound of knocking at the door,
The sound of sausages sizzling on the cooker,
The sound of bees buzzing,
The sound of balloons popping,
The sound of the phone ringing,
But most of all the sound of silence.

Sarah Young (12)
Deans Community High School

WORLD PEACE DAY

Children are dying,
children are crying.
Where is the happiness?
We once had a world with no shame,
we once had a world with no pain.

Bombs and guns and blood,
dead people lying in the mud.
Where does it end?
We once had a world with no shame.
We once had a world with no pain.

While we have our fun,
while they face a gun.
They have no hope.
We once had a world with no shame,
we once had a world with no pain.

We often live very long,
but soon after birth they are gone.
Give them some peace.
We once had a world with no shame,
we once had a world with no pain.

Lisa Burnside (15)
Deans Community High School

BETRAYAL

I already know, it's happened before -
Someone told me what they had seen.
I sit at home, wait by the phone,
Waiting for that silent call.
Will it show or shall I tell,
This suffering finish to my day.
Is it worth it or shall I regret,
The pain I wait for in my debt.

The door opens, it walks in,
A smile, a prance,
My emotionless face stares like a statue.
Searching her eyes through to her heart,
Her secret betrayal, it will not show.
She asks a question,
I will not hear,
For these next words are what I fear.

It's now all over, she has gone,
Disappeared, fading away like mist in the morning.
I cannot picture the pain of tomorrow,
Not to be there, living her moment,
I am too weak,
Can I go on?
This passion I loathe is much too strong,
I slowly pick up the phone.

Grant Begg (16)
Deans Community High School

THE SCHOOL CRITTERS

Sitting on your chair in
a big noisy room,
with teachers trying to disperse
the noisy critters,
who complain and
compromise with the teacher's
ruling voice.
They scream and laugh, and
have a good social life
unaware or caring
of the needs for the people more worthy
of the time,
the space,
the education.

Those critters,
those people who only wish
for a social life.
Day after day
they whistle
squeal and stand
in deserted parts of the school,
doping and squirming
at what they could make use of.

The critters,
the no-hopers,
whose only hope in life
is a miracle.
Those who would leave school
and lie on their beds
not caring,
not caring for a better way of life.
Not wanting a job,
only wanting money to indulge
in their habits.

Only caring for their own,
not caring
for the problems inflicted on others
by their school social lives.

Seniors,
a few types exist,
those who work
for a better way of life,
those who wish to gain
but have not
and
those critters
the layabouts,
the centre of the school
social life,
those annoying people,
those critters!

John Clelland (17)
Deans Community High School

GUESS WHAT?

There is a crashing.
The crashing is loud.
It is roaring and tumbling
and there is crackling under my feet.
A whoosh of air is in my ear.
Do not worry at all,
it is the beach!

Nicola Graham (12)
Deans Community High School

FRIEND OR FOE

Would you help me when I'm wounded,
Knock me out with an angry blow?
Would you tease me for the sake of it,
Are you friend or foe?

Would you watch me grow and be my friend,
Or bury my head in the snow?
Remove my foot with a mighty axe,
Are you friend or foe?

Would you give me a home if I get kicked out,
Or take the only joy I know?
Save my life if I almost die,
Are you friend or foe?

Would you save me, would you help,
Would you turn and run to go?
Would you kill me, would you sin,
Are you friend or are you foe?

Alison Parton (13)
Deans Community High School

THE SOUND OF WAR

Bang!
The gun goes off
Breaking the silence of the night.

Bang!
The gun goes off
And a man draws his final breath.

Bang!
The gun goes off
The man left to die alone in the night.

Bang!
The gun goes off
The sound of death and war.

Vicky McKenzie (13)
Deans Community High School

IRELAND

The Nationalists are fighting,
The Unionists want war.
Bombs are killing people,
There is lots of blood and gore.

There are sirens a-going,
The bomb squad's out again.
Many people could die,
If it wasn't for these men.

Our government is helping,
Ireland to stop the fight.
There have been a few ceasefires,
But it won't happen overnight.

Ireland will stop fighting,
Then Ireland will have peace.
When both sides stop arguing,
Then the war will definitely cease.

Fraser Cunningham (13)
Deans Community High School

SCHOOLDAYS

I sit in the classroom, right at the back,
thinking of giving the teacher a smack!

Who cares if one add one makes two,
I've got better things to do . . .

I'd rather be out in the hail and the rain,
than be stuck sitting next to the tutor group pain.

'Is 100mph fast or slow?'
Well frankly, dear teacher, I don't really know.

It's not really something I need to acknowledge,
especially since I'm not headed for college.

A job in Safeway is good enough for me.
Though lightening the load, isn't my cup of tea!

Jennifer McKay (13)
Deans Community High School

SPRING

The morning burst in through the window,
Like the crash of a little brother.
It leapt through the park screaming and shouting.
Spring ran through the town, dewing the grass,
Getting ready to enjoy April Fool's.
Little Easter eggs sit patiently in a shop window,
Desperate to be eaten by a very happy child.
The trees watch the rain fall,
And thirstily drink all the water.
It's not as cold outside and in the house,
The heaters announce, 'It's time for a rest.'

Linsey Lewis (12)
Deans Community High School

PRISON LIFE

Behind these bars I feel like
a caged mouse waiting.
I don't know when I am going to be tested
and I'm worried what will be the score.
Life behind bars, wondering
will I ever see my family again?
I feel sorry for myself,
bad dreams haunt me at night
and screams scare me.
Boredom fills my mind,
I know it's my fault.
I worry about my health,
anger and fear are my emotions
and I can't control them
I wish that things could be different
and the people in these cages beside me
would stop tampering with my feelings.
Then I realise it's not the monsters around me:
it's my conscience.

Gerald McGinnigle (13)
Deans Community High School

LAST TIME

It was a beautiful sunset
I wished it wouldn't end
But this was the last sunset
With my very best friend.
We talked and walked along the beach,
We were totally out of reach.
When out went the tide,
I knew I had to leave his side.

Charlene McGregor (13)
Deans Community High School

I LIKE NOISE!

I like the sound of the birds tweeting.
I like the sound of a horse eating.

I like the sound of a running river.
The sound of a storm to make me quiver.

I like the sound of a cat purring.
I like the sound of the washing machine whirring.

I like the sound of crunchy fruit,
I like the sound of snow beneath my foot.

I like the sound of a soft violin.
I like the sound of the sea waves' din.

I like the sound of falling rain.
I like the sound of a rushing train.

I like the sound of a mouse creeping.

But most al all . . .
I like the sound of my brother sleeping!

Lynsey McKeown (13)
Deans Community High School

WAR

People's lives taken.
People's lives over.
Violence on the streets,
But who has the power?

The terrible murders.
The violent war.
So what is all the
Conflict for.

Children crying.
They don't know
Why we are fighting.
So they hide down low.

What is it
This horrible war?
All these lives taken
But what are we fighting for?

Daniella Wood (13)
Deans Community High School

ANTICIPATION

I am the hunter, ever seeking
My prey in the darkness.
I can feel it, smell it close,
Even from this far I can taste its blood

In my Aquatic kingdom,
My prey cannot see me.
But they lie ever in anticipation,
Waiting for me to strike.

I lurk around in the deep.
I see its form looming out of the murk,
A shadow in the darkness.
Knowing not of my presence.

I strike fast as lightning,
A hurricane of air and blood.
A lifeless corpse floating.
Not a sound made or heard.

I swim in my peaceful world of darkness.

Ewan Hillary (16)
Deans Community High School

APRIL

April leaps over the hill,
Humming a song to itself,
Smelling the fresh flowers,
Bouncing, full of life.

Some greedy kids push by,
April falls, a startled cry.
The hill is empty,
Wind begins to roar,
April falls from the sky, lands at my feet.

Sun peers through lowering clouds,
April smiles, refreshed.
The wind ruffles the grass,
Warm and elegant.

Fragile eggs bumping, falling downhill.
Laughter pouncing on people,
Sun sleeping, moon waking.

Gemma Winchester (13)
Deans Community High School

LOST

I was walking through the forest with my family,
When all of a sudden they were gone.
I was as scared as a mouse face to face with a cat.
My head was spinning,
I think I saw a bat.

I sat down on a log and thought very hard.
I was so lonely it made me cold,
Though the summer breeze was lovely and warm.

Then out of the blue I heard a voice,
A familiar voice, a human voice.
I followed the sound, feeling brave.
I ran past gnarled trees, bushes and plants,
I came into sunlight and saw my mother's face,
And thought to myself, 'Thank God for that!'

Joe Triscott (12)
Dunbar Grammar School

TEACHERS

You walk into a room and sit on a chair,
You look up and they're there.
They come in all shapes and sizes,
And wear different disguises.

For at least 35 minutes a day,
They say they work for minimum pay
But all they do is sit in a chair,
And wish, wish they were elsewhere.

But we don't mind,
As long as we can find,
Time to expand our minds,
Or just sit and stare at the blinds.

Thin, fat, short or tall,
Green, purple, we've seen them all.
Don't laugh, giggle or shout,
Be careful there's detention about
And if down that road you do go,
Be careful you don't bang into the UFO
Because our teachers are a strange bunch,
They might just turn around and eat you for *lunch*.

Fiona Wright (12)
Dunbar Grammar School

SAD AND ALONE

Alone sitting there,
but do they care?
No one looks up
or gives a stare;
I wonder if they
notice that I'm
even there?

Feeling shallow and cold;
do they know what
I was told
about the deer and the toad?
The toad may have been old
But it wasn't ignored.

By the time they hear what I
have to say. It will be Sunday
morning and we will have to
go away and play.
Pray to the God of
Heaven and Earth
and thank him with
our trust after what
we have heard!

Kym-Clare McCoag (12)
Dunbar Grammar School

DOWN AND UNDER

Rising through the air like a flame from a fire,
Soaring through the sky like the blue in a rainbow,
Lying suspended like a smudge against the horizon,
Of blue and red and orange and yellow,
Which let the green-blue mass play its part,
Until falling away, silhouetting the sea of Cyan,
And hovering just before tearing the mirror of crepe paper,
Smashing the still sheet of glass,
Splintering and chipping the silvery mass of sunlight and blue sky,
Till entering the underground world,
With every colour more beautiful than the spectrum above
In the creatures down below of tropical fish, jellyfish and sea horses
Who greet the newcomer like a welcome banner,
And with one last contented glance at the heavens above,
The animal joins the other dolphins under the sea.

Catherine Ruth Fry (14)
George Heriot's School

SUNSET

The azure blue waves gently lap on my feet,
The sand between my toes as I look towards the heavens.
A blissful day was ending with a blissful sunset.
The warm, pink sky was growing ashen behind me in the west,
The sun, shimmering like a candle on the deep ocean waves,
Its glow sinking like a stricken ship.
As I bask in the final fleeting moments of daylight
Reflecting on a beautiful day,
Watching its fitting ending.
Nature's most dramatic spectacle.
As the world is plunged into darkness . . .

Ross G Alexander (13)
George Heriot's School

A Box

Imagine a box, not a very big one,
But containing the following indispensable items:
A television to watch and laugh at,
A James Bond film with action and adventure,
A photo album to remember times of past,
My happy family to love and to cherish,
My friends to crack jokes and keep me happy,
My cat purring loudly on my lap like a train,
My warm cosy bed to snuggle up in,
Imagine this box, which should not be too large,
Then take it and hide it with as little fuss as you can,
Somewhere you know its contents will be safe.

Finlay Long (13)
George Heriot's School

Snow

I crave for the white powder
Like I am addicted to it
For me it is like a drug
Although at touch it is cold and wet
It has an inner beauty of a different kind
I am not talking about an illegal substance
I am talking about snow
In the sunlight it glistens and sparkles similar to a diamond
The adrenaline rush I get from riding it
Is just short of ecstasy
For when I am snowboarding
I am on a continuous high.

Douglas James Crichton (14)
George Heriot's School

AS MORNING COMES

Thick and still it appears like it was a cloud.
It rests on the floors of alleyways and streets,
taking the plants and animals as its prisoners,
forcing everything it captures to stop . . . frozen.

As it moves the gales go too,
sweeping the pathways, searching
surrounding towns, villages
anything that lets it stay in power of the lands.

Then as morning swells
and when night turns to day
the rebellion comes to play.

As the strength grows, so does the beauty.
The dark, motionless tendrils which used to be,
are now coloured pink, white and green.

Now as the governor rises
he threatens the enemy with his powers.
The strong directs the opposition
who now struggles to keep his chair.

The end is near,
and as the fatigued commander fades away
he looks back and says,
'I will be back, when morning comes again!'

Jade Scott (13)
George Heriot's School

CHRISTMAS

The door opens and the children walk in,
Cold, wet but happy.
Outside stands their masterpiece,
Coal for eyes, a carrot for a nose.

The fire is burning,
Crackle, pop, crackle, pop.
On their mantelpiece are their stockings
Hanging just waiting.

Down one step, two, three, four . . .
The tree is glittering with a star on top.
Presents all around,
Under the tree, in the stockings.

Shake it, hear it rattle
What will be inside?
The paper is ripped off
A glee of delight.

The turkey is carved,
The plate full but soon nothing is left.
Dessert is next,
Christmas pudding, Christmas cake and mince pies to finish off.

Everyone is still sitting,
Crackers join everyone around the table.
Bang!
All pulled at once.

Everyone leaves with smiles on their faces,
Carrying big bags full of presents received.
Tired children, off to bed,
Climbing the stairs, one, two three . . .

Ruth Wilson (14)
George Heriot's School

WAR GAMES

Savage animals are sent into battle with
an unknown foe, for an unknown reason.
The battle is the middle of a tiger's gut;
no way out, no space, and all men are
claustrophobic.
The trenches are like spider webs
and all men are possible flies.
There is no safety from the screaming
birds of day.
Night brings the ominous, observant owls.
A challenge won is a challenge lost.
One day the deadly fog of war will come
to us all,
and then we shall perish
and finally the white dove will circle
the world without disruption.

Jamie Stewart (13)
George Heriot's School

A BOX

Imagine a box, not a very big one,
But containing all the following indispensable items
A photo of someone no longer here
A postcard from a friend on holiday
The flyer from that never to be forgotten concert
The special words from someone you love
The autograph from an actor
Your favourite song, remembered by all
Imagine this box that should not be too large
Then take it and hide it with as little fuss as you can
Somewhere you know its contents will be safe.

Laura L Pryde (13)
George Heriot's School

A BOX

Imagine a box, not a very big one,
but containing the following indispensable items:
An unopened present, a sun setting in a golden sky.
A Christmas carol in the snow.
A video without a cover.
A screwdriver set with some screwdrivers missing.
A brilliant novel with a twist at the end.
The laughter of a nation in tears.
The tears of a nation in laughter.
Imagine this box, which should not be too large,
then take it and hide it with as little fuss as you can.
Somewhere you know its contents will be safe.

David Hamilton
George Heriot's School

GOLD

Every year at the same time,
it starts.
The same winds, the same colours, the same bitter cold
And with them come the vast seas of gold and brown.
Every so often being whipped up by an invisible cyclone.

All but a few strong trees stripped of their colours.
They stand tall, like soldiers in battle,
Awaiting the gunfire of wind.
Their silhouettes stand ominously on the skyline,
With long knife-like branches,
Unsheathed by the wind.

Cameron Walker (14)
George Heriot's School

OAK TREE

It's as mighty as a bear,
on the inside.
It's as scabrous as a file,
on the outside.

It's as lush as a jungle,
at the top.
It's as desolate as a desert,
at the bottom.

The trunk is as packed as a market
near the ground.
The trunk is as slender as a piece of thread,
near the sky.

It's as pleasant as a tropical island,
in the summer.
It's as hideous as a toad,
in the winter.

It's as deformed as a country road,
higher up the tree.
It's as uninterrupted as a ruler,
lower down the tree.

Andrew Lamond (14)
George Heriot's School

RESTLESS NATURE

Like a roll of thunder from the bellows of the Earth,
A deep growl tearing through the peaceful night,
Pure power surging through the Earth's crust,
Spreading across terrain,
Like a plague in a slave's galley.
What is lacked in physical existence,
Is made up by sheer strength.
Nature's deadly monster at its worst.

The urban landscape is colossal in mass,
But compared to this ultimate force
Its size is worth nothing.
Once thought sturdy structures,
Crushed under the overwhelming power,
People streaming across buckling streets,
Like ants in their colony,
With the precise rhythm of a drummer,
The bombardment continues.

As the finale is drawn to an inevitable climax,
The ground squirms in its final death throes,
The motion is dispersed,
Leaving nothing but devastation and sorrow,
The silence grows louder.

Ben Rollinson (13)
George Heriot's School

WHO CARES?

It's early morning,
very early morning,
birds' whistles wake me up,
my radio suddenly bursts out for attention
and my mum bursts in,
'You'll be late for school.'
But who cares?

As the water trickles out
my eyes widen and my brain starts to tick
and suddenly I remember
'I have English homework.
Oh no!'
It looks like detention for me.
But who cares?

Squirt, squish, squash,
my gel slowly moves on to my palm,
I move it slowly and delicately through my hair
and mould it like one of Picasso's sculptures.
You could say my hair is modern art.
I do it to get the girls,
it never works.
But who cares?

I waddle into my car,
'Have you had your breakfast?' my mum squeals.
'No . . . I mean yes,' I say.
Gurgle, gurgle, gurgle my tummy rumbles like a sea dog,
I pray for a good day
But who cares?
Why do I bother?
But who cares?

Gregor Munro (14)
George Heriot's School

PURE WHITE

Look up and dream,
stare thoughtfully.
You see what you want to see.
Fluffy and baby-like,
pure white.
Parts of baby and dark blue all around.
With great eyes they watch
the world below,
like angels loving and caring.
You can never touch or keep one,
just watch them move around the world.
Sometimes they become angry and upset.
When they are upset, water will shower us in shame.
When they get angry, the effects are devastating.
They all sleep at night
but in the morning they rise
pure, white.
The angels are back to watch the world again.
Look up and dream.

Julie McCurdy (14)
George Heriot's School

AUTUMN

Summer has gone
and harvest time has passed.
Now fields lie bare,
their resting place at last.

The bales are stacked and wrapped
up in plastic by machine.
In olden days they stood as 'stocks'
a loved autumn scene.

And now, the leaves
are turning gold and red.
They gently fall,
and form a crispy woodland bed.

Spiralling smoke goes up,
from little cottage homes.
It's quiet now,
but what when winter comes?

Christopher Purves (14)
George Heriot's School

IMAGINE A BOX . . .

Imagine a box, not a very big one,
But containing the following indispensable items:
Your first love,
Your current love,
Your favourite film,
Your favourite song,
Your favourite moments
And the worst you learnt from,
All your best memories,
And the worst you can laugh at,
All this and still room for more, maybe . . .
Photos of all the good times to keep you smiling,
Maybe photos of the worst to teach you a lesson,
But in this box there is something very important . . .
All the good in your life.
Imagine if this box was yours.
Imagine a box which should not be too large
Then take it and hide it with as little fuss as you can,
Somewhere you know its contents will be safe.

Lisa Bolton (13)
George Heriot's School

THE MORNING

Ring goes my alarm,
as I tempt my fate,
in a cold shower is
something I hate.
Off with the drips
and on with the tie.
'Only toast for breakfast,'
I say with a sigh.

Up to the bus stop,
to stand in the queue,
I glance at the others
and spot somebody new.
Together we stand
in the cold, cold air.
We shiver once and then again,
it's really not fair.

Together the queue shuffles forward
As the bus comes into sight.
The driver is in a foul mood.
He shouts, 'Get your money right.'
Up the stairs we clamber,
to find a vacant seat.
Oh for a little more slumber,
oh for a little more heat.

At last we reach our destination
and down the stairs we rush.
I really don't know why we bother
for this place is really much worse.
It's noisy and old,
draughty and cold
but this is where my friends are
I like it here - it's quite bizarre.

Philip Purves (14)
George Heriot's School

IMAGINE A BOX

Imagine a box, not a very big one,
but containing the following indispensable items:
I'll live 'til I'm a thousand,
Blast off into space,
Have a game of football with an alien race,
Speak a universal language,
At school on computer,
Live on the moon, Earth, Mars or Jupiter.
Get the 4.30 rocket back to Earth,
Where all this began and the place of my birth.
We'll look back and open this box of mine,
And see what we thought in 1999.
Imagine this box which should not be too large,
Then take it and hide it with as little fuss as you can,
Somewhere you know its contents will be safe.

Craig Grieve (13)
George Heriot's School

CORFU

Plane descends,
Expectations rise,
Confusion circles the conveyor belt.
Transported through smells, heat and memories.
We drive through the busy coastal roads
Images from the window invade my consciousness
Attack my worries and concerns.

Standing on the wooden pier,
Gazing wistfully at the turquoise sea
My back is energised by the exhilarating sun,
Vitalised by its strength, I dive,
Flutter in the air for a moment
Then hugged by the warm refreshing water.

Never tiring I swim, dodge and play
Randomly floating,
Rocked like a baby in a cradle
Feeling safe and secure in the strong, undulating waves
Lapping against the beach
As the skinny cat laps her paws.

Idling on the balcony,
Savouring the holiday taste of Lemon Fanta.
When hungry, I eat
Summery tomato salad, bread, cheese
Hours float away in simple luxury

At night when all is still
Corfu reveals her beauty.
Sweet smelling stroll
Invaded by creaking of old crickets
More comfort than intrusion.

Homeward journey, like leaving a friend
Sad pleasure.
Better to rejoice in memories
Than to dwell in the past.
Back in familiar Scotland
Remembering feelings of warmth and comfort.
Corfu is part of my being and lives on in my soul.

Siobhan Foulner (14)
George Heriot's School

POWERFUL

It sat upon the table,
a wooden table with hundreds of wrinkles as if it was a
spiral, drawing it slowly downwards,
breathing bubbles through its thick lather of red, brewing slowly.
I felt its presence; powerful and strong,
it controlled my life.
It drew me in like a baby to candy.
The bubbles lay on top of the fizzy red, popping violently
like smashing windows.
It stares at me; hard and strong,
resistance was near impossible.
I knew it was waiting to strike.
It is a common part of life for most people,
but for some; it is a way of life.
It trickles down the back of my throat like water through a gutter,
flowing fast,
brings relief to most,
a hint of pleasure for those who drown their sorrows.
It changes your ways,
It changes your friends and it changes you life,
Until . . .

William Paul (14)
George Heriot's School

THE UNKNOWN

He is my friend
Oh yes he is
His eyes are big and piercing
Piercing like jagged icicles
His teeth are dazzling white, sparkling like little stars
He looks so gorgeous
in his coat of black satin
When he moves, his coat glides along his skin
following his every move
He is always looking out the window
like something found not lost
His feet are little padded ovals of velvet
His ears are always alert as if listening to our every word
He climbs our curtains
and falls down the stairs
Although so young and so little
He is my friend
My little friend
Oh yes he is
And that I know.

Rhian Reynolds (13)
George Heriot's School

WAR POEM

War is so terrible, full of destruction
Innocent people die and families are torn apart.
Missiles are launched demolishing cities
The sounds echo through streets, firing fear into every living person
Like the bullets from guns, fire death into people.

Bombs light up the sky like a fireworks' display
Only this one lacks the fun and enjoyment,
Soldiers are sent out to fight
Knowing that they are unlikely to return to their homes.

Buildings crash noisily to the ground,
Like the bombs dropped from planes.
Bodies are picked up from the ground
And thrown on to a heap like rubbish.

War is so pointless, a waste of time and lives
Millions are spent on bombs and missiles,
All that is gained is mass destruction and death,
And an everlasting hatred between the countries.

Greig Oliver (14)
George Heriot's School

THE BLUES

The slow, adagio music flies across you in the midnight breeze,
The saxophonist plays his heart out touching lightly on every key,
The slow, blue, magical words are sung to make people wonder,
How do they do it?

The miserable, depressing minor music makes you feel low and down,
The people are sighing with sadness and behind you children
are fast asleep,
Beside you, a couple are crying while the music makes you wonder,
Why do they do it?

The blue skies are covered by a blanket of navy and stars,
The moonlight shines on the wonderful band that plays,
Tears have welled up upon your eyes that is due to the music,
What is more wonderful than The Blues?

Ruth Rimer (12)
George Heriot's School

MEMORIAL BOX

Imagine a box, not a very big one,
but containing the following indispensable items:
the love of a parent,
the hug of a sibling,
the joy of a birthday, of Easter, of Christmas,
families, relations I treasure and cherish,
the lick of a dog affectionately,
the sadness of relations gone forever,
the dying of a special pet:
a gerbil lost in his peaceful sleep,
tears shed as I peer at these things,
not only in a box, but also my mind.
Imagine this box, which should not be too large,
then take it and hide it with as little fuss as you can,
somewhere you know its contents will be safe.

Emma Rigg (13)
George Heriot's School

IMAGINE A BOX

Imagine a box, not a very big one,
But containing the following indispensable items:
A fantastic family holiday,
The laughter of my friends,
The smell of a fresh summer's breeze
Brushing gently past my face,
The cheer of the fans, as I lift the trophy,
All the good times I have had,
The photos of friends and family that I keep dear to my heart.
Imagine this box, which should not be too large,
Then take it and hide it with as little fuss as you can,
Somewhere you know its contents will be safe.

Michael Thomson (12)
George Heriot's School

BEAUTY OR THE BEAST?

She is beautiful,
and powerful beyond our knowledge.
We like to think we know all about her.
We couldn't be further from the truth.

Inside her elegant
and perfectly sculptured body
she relies on every part of her
working to perfection.

We quench her everlasting thirst
in a hope she will serve us well
and she does, but at what cost?

She is as common as the cat
and is like it in many ways.
She comes in many forms,
colours and shapes.

She is not a mythical creature
and though we may not think of it now,
she will cause our demise.
She breathes out death.
Slowly but surely she is
letting a demon through to kill us all.

Callum Dryden (14)
George Heriot's School

IMAGINE A BOX

Imagine a box, not a very big one,
But containing the following indispensable items:
The first try for my rugby team,
The first match my team won,
My first real girlfriend,
A crazy little brother of four,
My PlayStation,
The first race I won,
The first words I spoke,
My first laugh,
My first smile,
Imagine this box, which should not be too large,
Then take it and hide it with as little fuss as you can
Somewhere you know its contents will be safe.

Peter Wyper (12)
George Heriot's School

SPARKLING SILVER

Crouched on the moss-covered floor.
Hearing a trickle of water,
spiralling down the neglected mountain.
Running in-between my dangling fingers.
A shiver is sent through my body
by the cool, fresh, shimmering water.
As I draw my hand in,
droplets of sparkling-silver drip off my fingertips,
and hit the glistening surface creating perfect ripples.

The immense height of bark soaring upwards,
then reaching a flush of arm-like limbs.
Splinters of light push their way through
the spiky old branches.
The light bounces towards the ground,
forming streaks of light in the dingy air,
which moves slowly through the winding trees,
to the world beyond.

Bianca Williams (14)
George Heriot's School

'THE BEAT GOES ON'

The tempo flows with your mood,
they way water flows with the river.
It relaxes you, soothes you
like rain falling gently against your window.
The beat can be steady like a ticking clock
or random like lightning in a thunderstorm.
It can fill in silences as if it knows the spaces in your life.

Lyrics reach out and grab you
like a lion pouncing on its prey.
They can tear you up inside
or can lick you smooth in a cleansing way.

The melodies can be very irritating
when stuck in your head.
Especially if they're ones that don't appeal to you.
It can energise and revive you
like indulging in a thirst-quenching
long drink after running for miles.

Music takes you into a world of your own.

Lauren Rodier (13)
George Heriot's School

The System

Born into certain inferiorisation
The only thing known: patronisation
One can only express individual ideas
When convenient to the overseers
Rebellious actions in the hope of justice
Just an excuse for further imprisonment
The system is a joke.

But the power will never be taken back
The 'have nots' are destined to suffer for all their years
Tormenting dreams of political power
But tomorrow hits with the harsh reality that
without the power to enforce a decision
They can't climb the rungs and rise above the
rank of 'common scum'.

Segregated by artificial respect
Some are blinded by the permanent stain of authority
Those who please can live in peace
But the ones who leave them discontent stand alone
At the mercy of those who are passionate about seeing them fall
Some play along or even endorse it
But most of them know the system is a joke.

Falsely assured of their importance
They patrol the field looking for trouble
If they fail to find some, they make it themselves persecuting
those involved
They probably know it themselves
They hide it because they're scared of it
Safe in the knowledge
The system is a joke.

Duncan Ibbett (14)
George Heriot's School

'POST TENEBRAS LUX'

I was happy and I became sad.
I was surrounded by people but I feel alone.
My smiles became cries.
My world was broken and my heart was empty.
The lovely bird became a horrible bat.
The bright sun became a terrible black hole.
'Where is the life in life?'

The people that I love, I hurt them.
The hopes that I made, I put it into a big ocean.
A huge dark ocean that everybody can start, but I'm the
                                    only one who can end it.
A huge ocean full of good things,
A huge ocean full of good people.
People and things that I am never going to see again,
Because I *threw* them.
I *threw* them, like someone can throw dirty clothes.
I *squashed* them, like someone can squash a fly
And I left them, like some leaves their cold soup.
'Where is the life in life?'

But one day I heard a voice.
The most beautiful and sweet voice.
It was the voice of a woman but sounds like an angel.
An angel, who came to answer my questions.
She saw me cry, she told me where the life in life was
And she brought me the light, the light of her kindness,
She showed me the sun; she showed me the bird,
She showed me the life, which opened my eyes.
But more than that
She gave me a reason to *live!*

Paola Cárdenas (16)
George Heriot's School

SHE

She lay there,
And let the morning rays of sunshine
Drift across her face.
She lay there,
With feelings of fear and excitement
Embedded within her.
The silence was shattered
By a harsh buzzing sound.
She moved, ever so slightly,
Only enough to listen.

Her heart started to beat faster,
With every taken step.
She felt dizzy, and slightly sick.
Her mother's voice,
Which was once clear as bells,
Was now only a faint whisper.
She started to hear another voice,
And snapped herself back to attention.
But soon she drifted,
Back to her own world.

She sat there,
Waiting, hoping, praying.
They had said it wouldn't hurt,
But as it punctured her skin,
She shivered.

They walked,
She thought.
They talked,
She remained silent.

She lay down,
She saw it,
The white liquid.
As it entered her veins,
She shivered.
Darkness.

She stirred.
She heard a voice.
A familiar voice.
A voice she knew.
A voice she loved.
She was safe.

Elaine Taylor (14)
George Heriot's School

A BOX

Imagine a box, not a very big one,
But containing these few indispensable items:
The smile of a baby showing all their joy,
The glory of a goal in the back of the net,
Getting an A in your latest report,
The happiness marriage creates,
And with these there are things, which must never be seen,
The sadness of the death of a grandma,
An argument which wrecked a good friendship,
The feeling of being dumped by a boy you adore,
Your team losing when once they were winning,
Imagine this box which should not be too large,
Then take it and hide it with as little fuss as you can,
Somewhere you know its contents will be safe.

Megan Forrester (13)
George Heriot's School

IMAGINE A BOX

Imagine a box, not a very big one
but containing the following indispensable items:
footsteps on a black night
the crunch of a sweet
the tedious click of a clock
the rattle of money in your pocket
the scent of a rotten egg
the popping of bubbles
a sulk from your brother
your own voice
the pattern of a snowflake
imagine this box which should not be too large
then take it and hide it with as little fuss as you can
somewhere you know its contents will be safe

Imagine a box, not a very big one
but containing the following indispensable items:
a pumpkin's smile
a Santa hat
school books
the first tooth that came out
a favourite teddy
the fairy from top of the Christmas tree
a musical instrument that you've played one too many times
a mouldy apple
imagine this box which should not be too large
then take it and hide it with as little fuss as you can
somewhere you know its contents will be safe.

Claire Oliver (12)
George Heriot's School

IMAGINE A BOX

Imagine a box, not a very big one,
but containing the following indispensable items:
a scorching summer holiday in Ibiza,
a New Year's Eve, partying all night,
the moment I became a brother,
my first day at school captured on camera,
my drama in primary school on film,
the wind against my face skiing down a mountain,
staying the night at my friend's,
the gold medal for a Scottish rugby tournament,
my relatives that have passed away.
Imagine this box which should not be too large,
then take it and hide it with as little fuss as you can,
somewhere you know its contents will be safe.

Jas Bruce (12)
George Heriot's School

MEMORIES IN A BOX

Imagine a box, not a very big one,
But containing the following indispensable items:
The change from puppy into dog caught on film
Postcards from friends disappeared to foreign lands
Tickets from old films
A gold medal Judith won skiing
The lost valley in the evening
Tara and Tufty playing on the beach
A dream
Imagine this box, which should not be too large,
Then take it and hide it with as little fuss as you can
Somewhere you know its contents will be safe.

Elizabeth Dyson (13)
George Heriot's School

THE BOX

Imagine a box, not a very big one
But containing the following indispensable items:
A picture that lifts your spirits when you are down,
The trinkets that remind us of those who have passed away,
The holiday the whole family was part of
And that you cherished every last minute of,
The summer sun breaching a forgotten beach and its rays
Casting its light over you and the emerald green sea,
The crunch of crisp autumn leaves as you walk down
The worn track by the canal back,
The lights of a Christmas tree on Christmas as the family
Is opening their presents,
The first bleat of a newly born lamb on a fine new spring day,
A successful birthday you and your friends shared in,
The happy days that everyone was part of,
The first game of rugby that you played in your life,
The time you became pack leader and led them forward,
All the sporting achievement you have done for your team
And the performance given,
Your brother's sixteenth and your sister's fifteenth,
All those good times,
Imagine this box, which should not be too large,
Then take it and hide it with as little fuss as you can,
Somewhere you know its content will be safe.

David Garden (12)
George Heriot's School

IMAGINE A BOX

Imagine a box, not a very big one,
but containing the following indispensable items:

warm thought, a cold smile
friendly face, an evil scowl
caring hand, a hard slap
childhood chum, a neighbourhood foe
lovely dream, a terrible nightmare
love letter, a suicide note.

Imagine this box, which should not be too large,
then take it and hide it with as little fuss as you can
somewhere you know its contents will be safe.

Fiona Blair (12)
George Heriot's School

NIGHT POEM

The moon is full, the stars are bright,
There's magic all around tonight.
I lie awake and wonder why
The stars stay put, in the dark sky;
And like a glowing balloon, that's lost its flight,
The moon just hangs, blazing bright.
It seems so secret, still and quiet,
As if pure silence raised a riot.
Except for the softly rustling trees,
All Earth seems to be at peace.
Mother Nature's cast her spell;
If the skies could talk, I'm sure they'd tell
Such wonderful myths and stories.

Jenny Allan (11)
George Heriot's School

A TRENCH TOO FAR
(The Great War 1914 - 1918)

In history you may well know,
There was a time of winter snow,
But not from the cold,
But from an event which would mould,
All of today.

It was a terrible thing to behold, is all I can say,
What mindless mediocrity and blinded rage,
That saw on the fields ten million die,
Either under a maxim bullet or the noxious fumes of a sly grenade.

To say the terrible truth,
That in all senses was aloof of humane expectations,
Was, and is still a world disaster,
Is and will be for years to come, a sad understatement,
                        as death could not have come faster.

Yes I know it was all in defence,
But surely reasoning would argue that revenge puts humanity
                                    in a fence,
For four bloody years, the mindless rage continued,
That made the world two fighting lions in a cage.

Retribution was dealt with savage intent,
Which brought yet more deaths to add another dent,
Into an already suffering world,
The war carried on, and one could find no grace,
For men of nerves of less than steel, or strength of less than stone,
This was not the place,
With every effort and utmost fear,
Did finally war succumb
To see a world in ruins and a Europe blazing with righteous fire.

Thomas Christopher Boston (12)
George Heriot's School

THE WANDERER

Through the early mists he comes, impartial,
He is as God but welcomes not one shrine.
He cares not for the land in which he wanders,
Not a wanderer of space, but one of time.

It has been said he does not like or loath us,
Indeed, his feelings died long ago.
He does not take an interest in our living,
Such things as hate and love he does not know.

He has been cursed with presence near immortal,
Though he does not live but only works.
His name is fear itself to our own people,
Though to death, round every corner sadness lurks.

Gabriel Brady (11)
George Heriot's School

IMAGINE A BOX

Imagine a box, not a very big one,
But containing the following indispensable items:
A boat sailing in its glory,
Some photos for which everyone has a memory,
A holiday at the seaside, or even abroad,
My grandfather and I holding his favourite fishing rod,
A photo of my friendship, for all the ocean's seas,
A day out very special to my friends and me,
My first words, aged one,
My first day at school and saying goodbye to Mum,
Imagine this box, which should not be too large,
Then take it and hide it with as little fuss as you can.

Kate Mackie (13)
George Heriot's School

A PLANE JOURNEY

The sound of footsteps against metal
As you hurry down the walkway and into the plane.
The thump of the bags
As they are placed in the overhead compartments.
The clicks and clanks as people strap themselves in.
The roar of the engines as you trundle down the runway,
Getting faster and faster.
The 'pop' in your ears and with a great big *whoosh!*
You're suddenly in the air, with the airport behind you.

The rattle of the trolley, bringing the in-flight meals,
The crunches and munches as you eat your way through it.
The talking and music of the in-flight movie,
The twinkling of lights in the cities far down below you.
The grunts and snores as people fall asleep (including yourself)
When you wake up, it's all a rush, rush, rush,
As you hurry to get everything tidied up and strapped in again.
Again, the 'pop' in your ears as you start to descend,
And suddenly with a *thump*!
You arrive at your destination
And the journey's over until another time.

Andrew H Mair (12)
George Heriot's School

CAT

I am summer, because I love the sun,
I am Egypt, as I am worshipped there.
I am the wind, swift and silent,
I am the bedroom, because I am soft like a bed.
I am no instrument, silent among my own.
I am a cat.

Scott Lumsdaine (13)
James Gillespies High School

THE LION

I am summer because I bathe in the sun,
I'm America, I've power over everyone.

I'm fire because of my mane,
When I attack, I'll inflict pain.

I'm a well-packed lorry,
Don't slack, you'll be sorry.

I'm the TV room, centre of attention,
I own a mansion, plus extension.

I'm a hammer, nailing you to the ground,
When I roar it's quite a sound.

My orange colour resembles the sun,
I roam about, I'll kill for fun.

I'm the ruler of the animal race,
Watch out or I'll wreck your face!

Joe Simpson (13)
James Gillespies High School

HYENA

I'm the street sweeper of the Savannah
I'm a jester, I'm a clown
I bring laughter to the grasslands
But people fear me in the towns.

My laughter's a death rattle telling
My prey to run away.

Until I strike and they see their final day,
For I am the jester and I always get my way.

Daniel McClure (13)
James Gillespies High School

EARTH

Earth
Small and insignificant
A dying planet amongst silent neighbours,
Surrounded by clouds of dust and acid,
Showers of liquid poison devastate forests and plains.
Billows of hot ash and molten rock spew forth,
Enveloping landscapes, destroying homes.
The great plates hoist and heave their colossal weight,
Clashing like titans, shaping the Earth and squashing countries.

Dwindling like a shadow,
Life holds on to a thread of reality,
Fighting off the destiny which threatens to drag it down
To nothing.

Calum Davey (13)
James Gillespies High School

TIGER

I'm a 4x4 because of my power, speed and agility, however,
I'm fire orange and charcoal black, I have stripes running
                                        down my back.
I'm as sharp as a knife. I have just taken a person's life.
I'm thunder and lightning. I'm very, very frightening.
I'm an assassin killing things for a living.
I'm big and strong, I do absolutely nothing wrong.
I'm the smartest animal of the jungle. When I'm hungry my
                                        stomach will 'rumble'.

Daniel Tracey (13)
James Gillespies High School

THE CAT

I am as black as night,
I have brilliant eyesight,
I see you when I'm in the dark,
Scratching about in the dark,
You can see me on the motorway in the dark
With my mysterious sighted eyes.
I have a very soft clean fur which I like to
Keep groomed all the time, so when someone
Touches my fur it is easy rub.
I like to play with you when you have
Wool in your hand.
I yawn like this so guess what I am . . .
And by the way my worst enemy is a dog.

Yasmine Mohammed (13)
James Gillespies High School

MY FAVOURITE SEASON

Guess what my favourite season is,
I bet you can't, I'll give you a clue or a few.
It's a time when the sun is always out,
When you lie on the beach forever,
No school to go to,
Seven weeks of freedom to do whatever you please.
Children screaming and shouting out loud.
Have you guessed yet?
I bet you have, I'll tell you then,
It is . . . *summer.*
So were you right?

Sarah Cathrine Murray (13)
James Gillespies High School

THE SEA

On windy days my waves fly high,
From my boat they touch the sky.

Animals like seals swim,
Eating fish,
The waves pass the boat rim.

When the sea is calm,
My boat gently floats,
And I try to steam away
From all the other boats.

When I take a swim,
My feet touch the slimy seaweed
And as I dive down deep,
I think of the expectations
Of which the sea excels.

Laura Davis (12)
James Gillespies High School

THE TURKEY

I live in a barn on a farm
So come along, have a peek at my beak!
I get a few frowns when people see my feathers are old and brown
My beak is shiny gold
Unlike my feathers which are old

So on Christmas Day I will not stay
I will be dead
And you'll be fed!

Jade McCabe (13)
James Gillespies High School

DRAGON

A flurry of fur
A glint of teeth
And then nothing
My prey leaves this mortal coil
Snared in my vice-like jaws

I am a beast
Hated and feared
Scales of shimmering sapphire
Great wings spanning fifty meters wide

I soar above ice-cold tundra
I soar above barren deserts
I soar above lush forests
Ever searching
Never finding

I am alone
Misunderstood
And alone.

Steven Penman (13)
James Gillespies High School

A PERSON I HATE

She is like the moody misty day.
She is horrible like jumping fire.
Her voice sounds like a nagging monkey.
Her eyes are evil as a hungry wolf.
She is a sour lemon.
Her voice is like a grumpy tiger.
Do I really hate her?

Amreen Haq (12)
James Gillespies High School

THE LION'S TAIL

I am autumn, fiery and crisp,
I am the fire of the jungle,
Smoke and a wisp,
I am the drum, my paws beat a steady rhythm as I stalk my prey,
I am the heart of the jungle, the night and the day,
I am the king, I am the queen,
My eyes are emerald, a fresh crisp green.

My mane is a wave of hot, red fire,
I'm sleek, mysterious, I'm one to admire,
Don't walk beside me, don't come too near,
The clash of my teeth is something you don't want to hear.

I love the jungle,
I love the trees,
But most of all,
I love me!

Kathryn Ritchie (12)
James Gillespies High School

BRAMA BULL

I hate the colour red, I rage with summer fire.

I am the timpani drum marching with elegance.

Mexico is where I live, it's always red-hot
and that is what you see when you look into my eyes.

I keep my two weapons in my hat, there like
two massive nails they cut flesh like butter.

Salman Iqbal (12)
James Gillespies High School

THE BROWN BEAR

I am winter, all frosty and cold
I am from the cold ice tops of the
Canadian mountains and the Alaskan rivers
I am fire, I am fierce, wild and strong
I am the kitchen, where I can eat everything
I am a hunter, working as the boss
I am a saw, tearing down everything I see
I make my shelters the best I can possibly do
I am a foghorn roaring out loud tunes
I am a big jumper, thick and woolly
But don't bother snuggling into me
I am the fighter, you cannot succeed
I've got lots and I want lots more
You see me here, see me there
You could see me anywhere.

Nikki Lunan (13)
James Gillespies High School

THE MILLENNIUM

When you say millennium
people think of parties and fun,
but ask yourself this:
Will the wars be over and done?
Will the famine be no more?
Will the drought still go on and on?
Will the injured ever be cured?
Will the scared be reassured?
Will the children still cry,
Or can we wave our problems goodbye?

Cara Anderson (12)
James Gillespies High School

FORBIDDEN

The car door slammed shut,
he realised his life would never be the same again,
he looked up at the sky,
why was it sunny on a day like today?

He walked inside,
big cumbersome doors,
shook and echoed,
the walls.

He sat down,
on the cold, hard stone,
his heart pounded,
and he shook,

he shook,
in the remainder of his life.
As he looked through
the cells at the life
he once knew.

Olivia Alabaster (12)
James Gillespies High School

WINTER

W is for the windy nights, that freeze your bones
I is for ice that's in ice-cream cones
N is for night-time when everyone's warm
T is for thanksgiving, the snowy storm
E is for enchantment, for Christmastime is near
R is for Rudolph, the red nosed reindeer.

Lindsay McRobb (14)
James Gillespies High School

ANCIENT HISTORY

Extinct, fossilised, large and small
Dinosaur

He is tough
He is durable
A shell from a cannon
A bullet from a gun
He is a bastion of hope
As he charges at the king
The T-rex appears
Gleaming with pride, high on the hill
Stopping in the arena
The arena of death
They stare each other out
I wonder if they realise
Their days may be numbered
He moved with ferocious speed
His horns white as chalk
They collide with tremendous force
One of them will taste victory soon
A blur, a cloud of dust
They emerged covered in blood, teeth baring
He let out a roar and collapsed
The victor emerged
Calm, cool, his horns covered with blood
The dinosaurs emerged
They bowed to their hero
And whispered
Triceratops, Triceratops, Triceratops.

Duncan Minto (13)
James Gillespies High School

SKIING

Skiing is my favourite sport
I've never done it in a port
I've been in the Scottish
Maybe I'll be in the British

I go skiing with the money I earn
I'd love to do a parallel turn
I go skiing in bizarre Hillend
The slope's so long I've never reached the end

I routinely travel to race training
When I'm there it always starts raining!
It is brilliant because it makes me go faster
I have never needed to use plaster.

Archie Liddell (14)
James Gillespies High School

LION

I'm raging fire, out of control.
I'm a hurricane that kills.
I'm the king of the jungle, strong and powerful.
I reign the animal kingdom.
No one will ever dare to overpower me.

My mane is fire.
My skin is golden sand.
My tail is a glowing splint.
My roar is thunder.

Cross my path and encounter hell!

Aishah Jabeen Akhtar (13)
James Gillespies High School

GUILTY CONSCIENCE

I'm the creek at the stair.
I'm the wind in the air.
I'm the never-ending scream.
I'm the eye with a stare.

I'm the crack of a window.
I'm the guilt in your heart.
I'm the blue in your mood.
I'm Picasso's art.

I'm the heart of your thought.
I'm the sought after thought.
I'm the black of the night.
I'm the guilty conscience in your mind.

Iqbal Zafar (13)
James Gillespies High School

A CAR

I am long and expensive,
I am uncontrollable.

I am different colours,
I am different shapes.

I have travelled the world,
My owners control me.

I am ever changing, I am ever here
I am a car.

Holly Benyon (13)
James Gillespies High School

TRANSFORMER

Alone
Different
Isolated from humanity

But now not different
Yet still isolated
The change has taken place

The people are scared
Though why I don't know
I yearn for humans
Flesh and company

I am seen
They scream

Werewolf!

Catriona Nichol (13)
James Gillespies High School

FEAR

I am unfriendly and unfair
and bleak with no calmness
I am dark and dangerous
and completely ominous
I hit you like stones and give you nightmares
I snare and glare and always
attack in the rain
You will laugh no more for you will scream
and I will laugh once more.

Jon McKean-Dow (13)
James Gillespies High School

A Spell To Make Edinburgh Sunny

To make Edinburgh sunny you would need the following . . .

1000 gold coins
A splash of human blood
An eye of newt
The liver of a blue whale
A gallon of human snot with a pinch of salt and the heart of Tony Blair
The brain of Maggie Thatcher, an ear of Boris Yeltsin and
A whole bottle of tomato sauce and
Coca-Cola from Tesco's
Double, bubble, toil and trouble, fire burn and cauldron bubble!

Lewis Burrell (14)
James Gillespies High School

Fire!

I am living in a match,
just one spark,
and I'm running all around.
People don't understand how the things I do
make the fire logs crackle and pop.
I kill, I produce light,
I'm the comfort in the night,
with only me you can see,
it's not worth the fight.
You'll never understand the things I do or feel,
but I am alive and I am real.

Sarah McBride (13)
James Gillespies High School

THE WHALE

I'm spring, nice and kind.
I'm the USA, big and strong.

I'm the wind, fast and hard.
I'm a dining room, big and fat.

I'm the boss of the hotel, I work for nobody.
I'm a pencil case and a pencil.

I'm a rocket, travelling the whole universe.
I'm the sea, nobody can dry me off.

I'm a locker, I keep lots of things in my stomach,
And nobody keeps me in a locker.

I'm a fisherman, I fish for fish and nobody fishes for me.
I'm a drinker, nobody drinks more than I do.

I'm the best footballer, I kick other creatures and
They cannot kick me back.

I'm a vampire, I bite other creatures
Then eat them and nothing will eat me.

I'm a cat, all other creatures are rats,
I get to catch them and they can never catch me.

Yin Fei (14)
James Gillespies High School

SECRET PARTY

Friends were in Germany,
Gone for two weeks,
We knew they would boast.
Something must be done.
We organised a party,
They wouldn't find out . . . ?
Party came,
We laughed but felt shame.
The doorbell rang,
They stood there . . .
'What are you doing?'
We stare in silence,
Caught in the act.

Sarah Wilson (12) & Karen Mackay (13)
James Gillespies High School

MIAOW

I am the hunter but I have no gun,
My teeth and claws are all I need,
Birds and fish are both my prey,
The glint of blood, the flash of claws,
Slash, slash, the bird is mine,
It's all over in a flash,
All that's left, a pile of feathers,
I may be small but don't hurt me,
I have relatives in high places,
My cousin is a king.

Owen Wilson (13)
James Gillespies High School

THE HAUNTING

I'm the shiver down your spine,
I'm the scream in the night,
I'm the laugh that breaks the silence,
During the howling night.

I'm the tear in your eye,
I'm the creak in the stair,
I'm the punch that knocks you out,
I'm the eyes that glare.

I'm the blood in your cut,
I'm the stab in your back,
I'm the teacher's frown,
I'm the witch's black cat.

I'm the spit in your face,
I'm the jokers grinning,
I'm the slam of the door,
I'm . . . the haunting.

Ross McBride (13)
James Gillespies High School

THE TIGER

My eyes are two emeralds burning in my head,
One look and you could be dead,
See them here and see them there,
My stripes are absolutely everywhere,
My ears pick up any sound,
Anything that scurries along the ground,
I used to be around a lot,
But now with the hunters, maybe not!

Jana Hunter (13)
James Gillespies High School

BRAVERY

As I ran down the battlefield
I could smell the blood from far away
And prayed to God to give me hope
Hoping as I pray!

As I got closer
I drew my sword
I felt freedom
I felt powerful
I swung the sword!

Sean Martin (13)
James Gillespies High School

THE DECISION

She crept down the corridor,
Checking for prying eyes,
Hesitated at the door,
Entered the room.
Once inside she bolted the door behind her,
There was still time to turn back,
Did she have to do it?
Did she want to know?
But fate decided for her,
Pandora opened it.

Susi Ebmeier (13)
James Gillespies High School

WHO MESSED UP OUR PRIMARY SCHOOL?

Who's to blame?
Who's the fool?
Who messed up our primary school,
With a messed up cloakroom with hats and coats all over the place?
Who messed up the cupboard,
With books, pencils and rubbers all over the place?
Who messed up the store room,
With brooms and mops all over the place?
Who messed up every classroom,
With tables and chairs upside down?
Who messed up our primary school?
Was it you?
Was it you?
Was it you?
You?
You?
You?

Rumana Begum (13)
James Gillespies High School

BRAVERY

B   rave are the soldiers.
R   aving down the battlefield.
A   s we get closer, the tension builds.
V   ictory is a soon awaited promise.
E   veryone is waiting.
R   evenge is sweet and in our eyes
Y   ielding to my sword, I run.

Edward Walls (14)
James Gillespies High School

HISTORIC SCOTLAND

Och aye the noo, och aye the nee, both don't mean much to me
All I know is that they are sayings and
Lots of tourists were paying
To hear these sayings said
All the tourists fled.
To hear these sayings said
But now they have completely gone and
Now practically dead.

Nessy, the great monster of the Loch
Why don't you move down to Leith Docks?
Then you could be seen
Or maybe you're just an imaginary being.

To the castle the tourists fled
To see the place where Wallace bled
Where Mary Queen of Scots gave birth
And the death of Alexander I on the Firth of Forth.

How stands Scotland the noo?

Jack Broussine (14)
James Gillespies High School

HAIR RAISING

If your head is bare
And you really care
When people glare
You could try a dare
To sort your hair
Try a spooky funfair
Your hair will rise with the scare!

Ryan McGonagle (13)
James Gillespies High School

HOMELESS

H omeless as the winter draws near
O n the street the homeless tremble with fear
M en and women search for food
E ver hungry in their search
L istening for people putting out their bins
E veryone thinks about their sins
S uffering people ask why, why, why?
S ilently people begin to die, die, die.

Tom Redpath (12)
James Gillespies High School

DARKNESS

D arkness takes away the light,
A nd makes the world out of sight.
R emoving the light from the sun,
K nowing colour is down to one.
N ot seeing the world like it's meant to be seen,
E verybody's life's covered by a screen.
S mokey black sky everywhere,
S eeing the world's darkest lair.

Ryan Lennie (13)
James Gillespies High School

THE FRIGHTMARE

It was cold, windy and dark,
on a cold autumn's night.
I was walking through a park,
and I saw a bat in flight.

Suddenly everything went blank,
and I was spinning in a twist.
But when I eventually stopped,
someone grabbed me by the wrist.

I looked to turn around,
and I got a massive fright.
There was a very ugly creature,
oh what a horrid sight!

He wore a long, black cloak,
and he looked a bit like clay.
I shouted 'Let me go!'
But he said 'You must stay.'

I didn't know what to do,
so I closed my eyes and screamed.
But then I suddenly realised,
that it was all a horrible dream.

Jamie Heseltine (13)
James Gillespies High School

CHEESE ON TOAST

C heese goes on top
H eat melts the cheese
E asy to make or cook
E asy to eat for yourself
S avoury
'E re we go

O ops-a-daisy!
N ot for long

T able to eat it on
O ff the table, boy
A h, here we go
S ugar, I burnt the toast
T omorrow I will have some more

Cheese on toast!

Thomas A Hutson (14)
James Gillespies High School

TRIVIAL TROUBLES

Now, someone worries about the colour of a dress.
Now, someone whines over their Gameboy not working.
Now, someone weeps in the dusty earth beside their family's grave,
patrolled by enemy soldiers,
surrounded by hatred and violence.
Now, someone mumbles, 'Shame,' in a comfy chair,
'Change the channel, bit depressing.'

Sophie McCabe (13)
James Gillespies High School

WHY IS THE SKY BLUE?

Why is the sky blue?
Why is the grass green?
Why does she have to be so mean?
But why do birds fly?
Why do fishes swim?
And why whenever I try to say something
she makes me feel all grim?
Why do people get married?
Why do they say 'I do'?
The only place I can really hide is in the girls' loo.
Why do we wear clothes?
When did it all start?
I'm sure she's a nice person at heart.
Why do people have emotions?
And why do we love and hate?
Is this deliberate or is this just fate?
Why do people become ill?
Why do we die?
Why do we tell the truth and why do we lie?
I wish people would understand,
I wish there were few,
That's why I am different,
I cannot help it,
And I wish I knew.

Kezia Lewis (13)
James Gillespies High School

Potion For Good Looks

Fillet of a fenny snake,
In the cauldron boil and bake,
Eye of bat, and toe of dog,
Wool of lamb and tongue of frog,
Adder's fork and big bee's sting,
Lizard's leg and small sparrow's wing,
For a charm of dazzling good looks,
Mix it well until out come spooks.

Adam Perry (12)
James Gillespies High School

Starfish

S itting on a rock at the bottom of the sea
T hinking what to do
A ll alone and bored
R emoved from the rock by the tide
F loating across the ocean
I n the middle of nowhere
S inking slowly
H itting the seabed.

Duncan Fraser (12)
James Gillespies High School

CRAZY TEAM

Kilmarnock is a crazy team
Old men from other clubs
When there has been a lot of rain
They send on all the subs

They do not have a big support
Nobody ever goes
Unless the Celtic come to play
Or even the Blue-Nose

The team and pitch are very funny
The ball goes the wrong way
But even then they score some goals
To earn their weekly pay.

Steven Donoghue (15)
Kingsinch School

KINSHIP

The yelling, the wailing, the screaming in rage,
These are the noises which come from each cage.
The thrashing, the snarling, the last pleading din,
Why must they torture my beloved kin?

They say it is necessary, they say that they must,
But I know it is only the blood that they lust.
The lethal injections that pierce the skin,
Oh, why must they torture my beloved kin?

But listen my darlings, please do not fear,
There are those who care and shed a tear.
And until mankind sees its horrid sin,
I will stay by and protect you, my beloved kin.

Laura Fraser (14)
Portobello High School

WHAT I HATE

What do I hate? I hear you ask,
What do I hate? What an endless task,
I hate it when the sun goes down,
Upon my face it leaves a frown,
I hate it when I have to work,
It makes me feel like a great big jerk,
I hate it when I go to school,
'Cause everyone makes me a fool,
I feel like I have to scream,
When you're at school you have to seem -
Like someone who has to go!
I wish they weren't so slow you know,
I have to let out my hate somewhere,
Otherwise I'll end up ripping my hair,
I feel so tormented when I'm at school,
Everyone has to be so cool,
I hate it when they make fun,
Mind you their brains are close to none,
Still I hate it every day,
I always have to slave away,
To walk about the school playground,
I hate it, what a horrible sound,
I guess I have to say it now -
I don't know why, I don't know how -
But I suppose school's . . . not that bad -
Even though, it is quite *sad!*

Sarah Kwan (13)
Portobello High School

ME AN' MA PALS

Here a am, sittin' in ma hoose,
Wi nowt tae dae, starin' aboot.
A luik oot ma windae, sittin' alane.
A'm on ma tod, naeb'die's oot.
A'll gie ma pal a phone,
Hae a wee natter
Ma ma'll moan aboot the bill -
Och, that disnae matter.

Weel, that's that done,
Caught up on the goss.
She's invited ees oot,
Dinnae forget the lip gloss!
We're gaun tae Porty,
Doon tae the shows.
Whit time A'll get hame at
Naebodie knows.

Whit a guid laugh we hud,
Me an' the crowd.
We got chucked off the waltzers
Fur bein' sae loud.
A'm gaun awa' hame,
A'm knackert, A'll get the bus.
Cup eh tea, bit eh toast,
An' a shower's a must!

Natalie O'Loan (12)
Portobello High School

MIST

As I look around me,
I see the damp mist,
Drooping down over me.
It is cold and damp.
It is not as cold as winter,
And not as wet as rain,
But it is a mixture of those things that make it so
Depressing, lonely and mysterious.

It is clinging onto my clothes,
It is trying to tell me something,
But what could it be?
Could it be a secret,
A secret it has held for years?
Maybe it is a crime it has seen,
But cannot tell.
Maybe it is a cry for help,
Pleading for attention.
Seeking for an answer,
Seeking for an answer about life.
I feel like it is asking me why we fight,
Why there is so much war and hatred in this world.
It moves on and on trying to find this answer,
Taking all its secrets with it.

Will it ever find the answer?
We will never know.

Gillian Vesco (13)
Portobello High School

FAIMLIE OOTINS

Here we go again,
Divin' aboot daft,
Makin' pieces,
Fillin' flasks.

It's a faimlie ootin', ye see,
W ma Ma, ma Da an' me.
We're gaun tae Peebles,
An oor in the car -
A dinnae ken hoo we can gae that far!

Finally, we get there
Straight intae the water.
A cuidnae be mair hotter.
There's a giant hill in front o' me.
Climb it! ma Da wuid say.

Time tae gae hame.
Exhausted, A am,
Gaun hame, rare an' calm.

Thank guidness that's owre.
Nivver again am A gaun on a
Faimlie ootin'!

Samantha Brockie
Portobello High School

THE MEETING

The foghorns were a-blowing,
Waves smashing and bashing,
There I wait and waited, waiting,
For anything the magpie claws,
Along the misty horrid shores.
Two eyes staring at me catch my glance.
The face is familiar,
Like a page in a book,
She calls my name softly like a flute.
A gift from heaven, sent from above,
Glossy hair sways with shining blue eyes.
Her clothes are old fashioned with a hoop in one hand,
Shaking my head I walk away,
Old Granny Paton alive again.

Alison Freeman (14)
Portobello High School

COOL TO BE CRUEL?

When I was just a child of five,
I'd love to see animals so alive,
When I was just a child of six,
I'd play with my dog to get my kicks,
When I was just a child of seven,
I swear, I cried and cried,
For I found out the truth about the world,
When I learnt that some animals get fried!
They die for your bacon, they die for your mince,
That's why I've been a vegetarian,
Ever since!

Stacey Lee Drew (12)
Portobello High School

JAGUAR

In the rainforest lies a jaguar,
laying by the waterfall alone,
It roars for attention but nothing will come,
Why is this such a lonely beast?

It searches for food, but nothing is to be found,
When it sees something moving on the ground,
It walks along slowly, cunning and careful then,
It starts getting faster and faster, faster and faster,
When suddenly,

Boom

The jaguar is not alone now,
And I'm not going home,
I felt really sorry for this beast,
Until it made me its lunch time feast.

Lauren Banks (12)
St David's High School, Dalkeith

SOMEONE SPECIAL

My nana is my guiding light
A shooting star across the midnight sky
Her eyes sparkle like gold and an angel she is in my heart.

Stories she knows that need to be told
She tells us with pleasure and pride
My nana sends me so many gifts from her heart
All wrapped up in love.

Laura Herriot (12)
St David's High School, Dalkeith

One Winter's Afternoon

One dull and foggy winter's day,
my friends and I went out to play.
The snow was white, the sky was navy,
inside - turkey, potatoes and gravy.

Sledges out, slide down the hills
it really is great fun.
We're full of energy, ready to go,
we're really on the run.

We've had enough of that for now,
we'll move on to something new.
We'll make a snowman, that'll be good,
we'll make it out of snow and food!

The snowman's ready, standing tall,
beside the door and the hall.

It's really cold, time to go in,
we have our Christmas dinner.
The next day we go out again and
find a pile of snow, a great big puddle, a carrot.
He's never coming back!

Carrie Cunningham (12)
St David's High School, Dalkeith

Summertime

As the birds sing in the trees,
As the children play on freshly cut grass,
As the sun's rays beat on my skin,
I think this is why summertime is so much fun.

Scott Galbraith (13)
St David's High School, Dalkeith

THE PLAYGROUND!

The playground deserted, all alone,
There's no one out to play.

Empty crisp packets lying,
Buzzing wasps in the bin,
Squawking seagulls flying round and round to see what they can win.

Soon it's home time,
Noisy children bursting through the doors,
Running out to the playground which they truly adore.

Mothers waiting for them,
To take them home,
Now the playground is all alone again.

Next day, playground busy,
Shouts and screams from children,
As merry as can be,
But then the early bell goes,
Playground silent again,
Silent, while the children work.

Suzanne Rankin (11)
St David's High School, Dalkeith

COLOURS

Yellow is the colour of the shining sun.
Blue is the colour of the wavy sea.
Green is the long green grass growing in my street.
Silver is the fish shining in the deep ocean.
Black is the darkness in the sky.
Nothing is when I close my eyes and drift into a deep sleep.

Donna Edie (13)
St David's High School, Dalkeith

SCHOOL

On a bad day
School is . . .
A prison,
Guards shouting
Words,
Words you don't understand.
Forced to stay,
All day.

On a good day
School is . . .
A family,
My family,
My friends,
My life.

Laura Gillies (12)
St David's High School, Dalkeith

SNOW

Fluffy and white,
Cold and wet,
Snow is fun to play in.

Building snowmen,
Snowball fights,
Big hills are great for sleighing.

Snow comes at Christmas,
You get into the mood,
When the snow is falling.

Lisa Hume (13)
St David's High School, Dalkeith

THE SEA

The motion of the waves
Seagulls flying, crying
Crashing waves hitting hard
Stop!

Calm
Dripping of rain hitting the waves
Heavy drips hit the water
Feel the waves take the pebbles with them to the sea.

Suddenly, stop!
The barrier halts the waves
Rainbow flies across the sky
Beautiful red, blue, green
Pink, purple and orange
Sun appears
Sea is calm.

Sarah Grealis (12)
St David's High School, Dalkeith

THE COOL CAT!

The cool, calm cat
With bright amber fur
Is slowly slinking
Through the long, green-yellow grass,
Hidden, only his 'Miaow' can be heard.
He comes pounding up to me,
Pleading for attention. His fur is so soft and fine.
Suddenly! He bounces away,
Over the fence, not to be seen again.

Andrew Nicolson (12)
St David's High School, Dalkeith

THE GLOOMY WINTER WOOD

The gloomy winter wood is as cold as ice,
You could never describe this wood as nice.
The trees just drape, slump and hang,
You'd never know that the birds once sang
In this grey and lifeless wood.

The bushes are black, or brown, or grey,
This is no place where the birds would stay.
You can hear the swishing of the leaves,
On the dark, dark gloomy trees
In this grey and lifeless wood.

Then the snow falls, so heavy, so thick,
On the dark grey branches and sticks,
Then the white dissolves away
And the spring-summer sun comes out to play
In this beautiful fresh spring wood!

Jennifer Griffin (12)
St David's High School, Dalkeith

A DULL WINTER'S DAY

In the winter it is cold
and the ground is
filled with snow.
The trees are white and
so is the grass and
cars can't get up the hill.
It is gloomy and dull.

Lee McNeish (13)
St David's High School, Dalkeith

THE FUN IN THE PLAYGROUND

The children are laughing and crying,
They are having fun, jumping, skipping and eating.
Their mums have packed their play piece.
Will it be fruit or crisps?
Fresh orange or Coca-Cola?

The bell has rung, everyone is excited,
But some are angry.
They didn't put their rubbish in the bin.
The crisps, juice are all around.
The children are in their lines,
Ready to go into their class.

Ashley McFarnon (12)
St David's High School, Dalkeith

BOOM, BOOM

Boom, boom, the punches go
as they land on the boxer's nose.
The coach is cheering him on but
jab, jab, the boxer is down.

Round two is about to start
as the boxer is about ready
as the other boxer is about out.

Jab, the boxer is down
uppercut, the boxer is dazed about the place
hook, hook, hook, the boxer is out.

Gary Miller (12)
St David's High School, Dalkeith

UNTITLED

The playground is my favourite
Place at school
With lots of people and
Lovely smells like Coke and crisps.
I hate the bucket with
The wasps around it, the evil buzzing.
I love the chance to
Eat and play - crisps, hide and seek.
You can do it
Either way.
I love the sun, I love the rain
I'll go out whatever it is.
The playground is my favourite place
At school.

Nicola Niven (12)
St David's High School, Dalkeith

GINGER

Union Jack and ginger hair,
Ginger Spice what a scare.
There were five but now
They're four - there's no Ginger anymore.

She sings with her heart on a lonely stage,
Sometimes in kindness and sometimes in rage.
'Take me back!' I could hear her sing,
She waits by a phone that never rings.

Vikki Hamilton (13)
St David's High School, Dalkeith

THE TREE

The old tree stood,
Silent, dark.
Just a thick layer of wood,
Covered in rotting bark.
Rustling in the wind,
The little leaves it had.
'How long has that been there?'
One day I asked my dad.
'Many, many years,
Before I was born.'
The tree was an eyesore,
Standing in the street.
Until one day, it was gone,
Just a tree stump left as a reminder,
Of that old, old tree.
Missed only by my dad and me.

Fergus McGlone (12)
St David's High School, Dalkeith

THE WINDOW

Look out of the window and see what's there,
Trees, houses and hills in the background, what a beautiful sight.
All the leaves off the trees, listen carefully and you'll hear,
Whoosh and hiss as the wind blows.
The birds in the sky flapping their wings at great speed,
And all the people out playing with happy smiles on their faces.
What a view from out the window.

Eamonn Reynolds (11)
St David's High School, Dalkeith

TITANIC

The ship of dreams,
everyone thought it was but it was not.
It hit an iceberg on that cold winter's night
and then it sank out of our sight.

People shouted,
women and children,
but it was so cold and there were
thousands of terrified people screaming.

Help arrived but there were few who survived
and then it all went silent.
Not a voice to be heard
just the crashing of the freezing cold waves.

Steven Rose (11)
St David's High School, Dalkeith

THE SEA

The sea is a cold place, damp and wet,
The howling of the wind like Pavarotti,
Waves crashing like drums,
Crabs, insects scuttle for shelter,
Kids cold, hugging their mums.

The sea is a hot place, sun and sand,
People bathing, swimming, making angels in the sand,
Eating ice-cream, having fun,
It's good at the sea when there's sun.

Ian McManus (12)
St David's High School, Dalkeith

AFTER A HORROR FILM

Silence is surrounding me,
A horrible feeling you are *not* alone.
You get nervous - are you sure no one is there?
Was that a creak from the floorboards upstairs?
Did I hear someone else's breathing?
I'm getting myself all worked up.
Oh hurry someone please come home.
Was that a door creaking?
I tiptoe quietly making sure *I am alone.*
Was that a scrape from the cupboard under the stairs?
I open the door so slowly that I am filled with fear, until . . .
Boo! Aaahh!
The bogey man!
Oh! It's just my little brother.

Nicola Rowan (13)
St David's High School, Dalkeith

LOVE

Love is a very strong word
Most people think they know what love is
But they don't
You will never know what love is
Until you experience it
On TV you think you see love
But it is all fake
Some people imagine their true love
Mostly girls I have to say
But when we do fall in love
It will be nothing like you thought it would be.

Gary Dickson (13)
St David's High School, Dalkeith

FEAR

Walking alone through the forest,
I hear the rustle of leaves in the sharp cold wind,
Small animals scurry across the forest floor,
Owls hoot.

I hear footsteps behind me,
I swirl round,
A black figure dives into the bushes,
Fear sweeps over me, I can't think straight,
My heart beats in my throat.

I walk faster,
The footsteps quicken with me,
I run,
The footsteps run,
Twigs snapping,
Leaves crunching, bushes rustling,
The trees tower over me,
Suddenly I'm falling, falling . . .

I wake up,
It was just a dream,
Then I look at my hands,
They're covered in mud.

Sara Toule (12)
St David's High School, Dalkeith

THE DOLPHIN

The dolphin is an intelligent creature,
That swims gracefully through the sea,
Looking for some fish to eat up for his tea.

The creature is so friendly,
Friendly as can be,
It likes its strokes and pats from you and loves the ones from me.

The noise it makes is loud and high,
It almost reaches to the sky,
Its bottled nose and crystal eyes
Are as clear as the brightest bluest skies.
Its smooth grey skin is as rubbery as can be,
I love dolphins as you can see!

Lyndsay Wyse (11)
St David's High School, Dalkeith

BASKETBALL

Bounce, bounce the noise of the basketball goes
All around the court,
Score yes, 2 to us.
Keep the ball going,
Everybody tries to catch it,
To and fro it goes,
Backwards and forwards there it goes,
All around the court.
Left and right you dribble the ball,
Left then right we score.

Lee-Anne Partenheimer (13)
St David's High School, Dalkeith

ON THE BUS

The wheels on the bus
go round and round.
Our bus driver is very sound.

Sitting on the bus
everybody there screaming
and pulling at their hair.

Some people are quiet
some people are loud
we don't care because we aren't in that crowd.

Up the stairs is so quiet
up the back I always sit
that's where all my friends are at.

People eating, people drinking
people picking their noses
people running up and down
people fighting.

At the end of the day
everybody runs for a back seat
and it all starts again.

Keith Barr (12)
St David's High School, Dalkeith

OH NO, IT'S HER!

I looked at my timetable
I knew what was near
It was my one and only fear
I had *her!*
I was waiting at the door, sweating and panting
Out she came looking for her victims
Smelling out their fear
She's ready to pounce
As soon as she gets the chance
I talk to my friend, saying she's, she's short and stumpy
Then she shouts out loud
'Stay back after class'
Shivering as I said it
I replied 'Who me?'
She said 'Yes, you.'
I knew I would dread it
I could taste my worry
Then the bell went and everyone ran out
She said 'Do you know why you've been kept back?'
I was too scared to reply
She laughed and said
'To clean the blackboards. I bet you were scared.'
I was so pleased
I thought maybe she's not so bad.

Andrew Clarke (12)
St David's High School, Dalkeith

YELLOW

Yellow is the colour of summer,
The colour of happiness around.

Yellow is the colour of the sun
Which warms us up each day.

Yellow is the colour of the fields
Which the daffodils and sunflowers grow in.

Yellow is the colour of the shirt
That the man wears down the street.

Yellow is the colour of my little sister's raincoat
When she goes out in the rain.

Yellow is the colour of the fruit
That is very sour.

Yellow is the colour of the paint
To paint my lovely flower.

Sunbathing in the sunshine with lemonade to quench my thirst
And a yellow banana to keep me going.

Yellow is a warm, happy colour!

Ruth Clarke (13)
St David's High School, Dalkeith

RAIN

Rain comes pouring down
Making all of these sounds
Splish, splash, dish, dash

Rain, rain, everywhere
If it's raining it's always there

When it's raining, it's always wet
Like gel on your hair waiting to set

You can tell between
The different rains
Normal rain pelts
Acid rain melts

But this is what I
Like about the rain
It's cold, it's clean
And it's always wet.

Matthew Coyle (12)
St David's High School, Dalkeith

GOLD

Gold is so shiny,
Gold is so sparkly,
Gold is my clock that goes tick-tock,
Gold is my hair, well if I am lucky,
Gold was my ring but now it's all yucky,
Gold is the sun so very, very bright,
Gold is the best, it fills me with delight.

Tracey Moffat (13)
St David's High School, Dalkeith

SUMMER HOLIDAY

The bell rings - it's summer!
Get your lunch,
Phone your pals,
Swing on the swings,
Then wrap them up.

Get our bikes,
Go down the wood.
Rally them to the golf course.
Look for some balls, then get our bikes,
Go back to the park,
Unwrap the swings,
Then go for our tea.

Go on our holidays then come back
Phone our pal, get down the park.
Go swimming all day long.

Last day of the holidays
Can't wait to get to see your friends
Tell them about your holidays
Then the bell rings - oh no, it's English!

Marc Dickson (12)
St David's High School, Dalkeith

MY DOG!

Small and brown,
Cute and funny,
Her coat almost the colour of honey.

She's friendly and happy
And she loves her food - Chappie.
Chappie smells like rotten eggs,
She likes it though, when she sees it she begs.

My dog also loves going for walks,
When she sees her leash she talks.
She loves running around
And rolling in poo on the ground.

If she sees a rabbit or hare
She'll be away.
You can shout but she doesn't care,
She'll not come back for a while anyway,
But when she does she's dead for the day!

Paul Fitzsimmons (13)
St David's High School, Dalkeith

IN THE MORNING!

I get up at 7.30,
feeling really sad,
I think of skiving school,
bad then I would be, bad.
When I get out of bed,
I go down for my towel.
When I switch on the shower,
it all comes out with great power.
I get dried very quickly,
then I clean my teeth.
I get dressed in my room,
I go to school very soon.
I leave the house at 8 o'clock,
go in for Steven, round the block,
I ring the bell,
he opens the door,
the day's not mine,
anymore.

Matthew Glynn (13)
St David's High School, Dalkeith

THE BERMUDA TRIANGLE?

Bermuda Triangle what is it?
Is it a portal left by a UFO?
Is it one of those phenomenon?
We will never know! There's
Been lots of people who say
That it is a sea monster and
The rest say it's a hoax.
The first ship to disappear
Was one of Christopher
Columbus's ships, another
Case was twelve bombers who
Flew into it and didn't return so
They sent another bomber and
That too disappeared, twenty-four
Pilots were missing so this
Phenomenon might have been by
UFOs, How do I know?
Because I am an alien!

David Thomas (13)
St David's High School, Dalkeith

GREY

Grey coating the dark foggy clouds.
As grey as my teacher's hair.
My neighbour's grey car speeding round the dodgy corner.
The cat strolls along the road with its grey shedding hair.
My grey pencil moving along the page as it
Copies down my punishment exercise.
An angry teacher looking at me through her light grey glasses.
Grandad baby-sitting me with his old grey trousers on.
The grey stormy waves crashing through the water.

Rosina Marr (12)
St David's High School, Dalkeith

THE SEA

The sea at the beach is noisy,
Hearing the waves crashing on the rocks.
Waves blowing along the blue sea,
Sea right up upon the sand.
Pebbles blowing along with the waves,
Is that seaweed I can smell
Floating on the water?
Shells all different colours,
Blue, yellow, orange,
Scraping along the sand.
The sea is blue,
Light blue, dark blue,
Moving in the water.
The wind blowing hard and strong
Making the sand move fast.
Waves splashing, crashing everywhere,
Waves big or small still make a noise
As it hits the sand.
Wind making shells scrape faster
Along the sand.

Emma Rattray (12)
St David's High School, Dalkeith

THE TREE OF LIFE

Tall as the sky,
It spreads out its wonderful arms of life.
A blanket of leaves spreads across each branch,
A home for birds and animals.
It gives oxygen which we need to survive.
A golden shower of leaves falls with each breeze.
It looks down on everyone like a guardian angel in heaven.

Lyndsay Paterek (13)
St David's High School, Dalkeith

THE GOLDFISH

The goldfish is orange with black spots,
It has a giant triangle shaped tail,
Two small beady eyes,
A small red mouth with black fins,
And lots of gold scales.

The goldfish glides along the surface,
And in and out the waves.
It chases its food before eating it,
Sometimes it comes right out the water,
It acts like a shark.

The goldfish floats smoothly all around the tank,
It goes in and out the tunnel,
And gets lost in the reeds,
The goldfish is happy.

Russell Kyle (13)
St David's High School, Dalkeith

FAME

Ten thousand screaming fans shouting out my name,
I sing,
I dance
As I look over the electrifying crowd.
They're so loud,
I feel pride,
'We love you,' they scream.
Adrenaline runs,
Sends my head reeling,
What a feeling!

Katie Main (13)
St David's High School, Dalkeith

MONDAYS

As I walk through the gates in the morning,
And hear the chatter of the shy and anxious 1st years,
I know I have a busy day ahead of me,
With a burden on my back!
Monday mornings
As I enter the building,
I get pushed about by the higher years, showing off,
I try to spot my friends,
But can only see teachers, half asleep with bags under their eyes.
Monday mornings
I sit down on a chair and fall into a gaze,
I dream about my bed as if I could almost touch it and hop right into it.
Monday mornings
I smell the distant scent of food rising in my nose,
As my tummy begins to rumble, I can almost taste it,
Missing out on breakfast seems a bad idea now.
Monday mornings
I jump up and am suddenly alert.
The piercing scream of the bell, penetrating through my brain,
Everyone begins to move causing a traffic jam in the corridor,
Oh, this is such a pain.
Monday mornings
I drag my feet to the next class,
I really don't think I can last,
A whole wasted hour still left to go,
Oh I really can't wait to get out of here and go home!
Monday afternoons.

Lauren Arthur (12)
St David's High School, Dalkeith

WHICH ONE?

Looking, looking which one will I pick?
I can't have a rat, they make Granny sick.
I don't want a goldfish, they just go round and round,
But I could get a puppy, a little grey hound.
My mum said, 'No, they lose too much hair,'
She'd have to clean up but that's no way fair.
I could get a hamster, no they do not last,
Or a little cute gerbil, no they are too fast.
I could get a budgie and just call it Bessy,
My dad said, 'No they're far too messy.'
'There is no hope,' I said to myself, then
I started to cry which is bad for your health.
I lay in bed and thought half the night,
'Am I ever going to find the one that is right?'
I went out in the morning, there she lay,
As beautiful as a beautiful day,
I went to stroke her white, silky fur,
And then I fell in love with her!
A wonderful rabbit, the best of the best,
She is more wonderful than all the rest!

Heather Stafford (13)
St David's High School, Dalkeith

MATHS

Numbers, numbers, numbers,
They're all jumbled up,
They're all scrambled up.
The smell of the new books,
Me chewing my pencil,
Oh they're all muddled up.
Where do I start
The left or the right?

Pythagoras who are you,
Some nutter who invented squared and geometry?
What is squared?
What is geometry?
Squared is squared,
Geometry is something to do with triangles,
Well that's what I've heard.
Algebra - you sound so pretty but you're . . .
eSomething about x2+3=8.

Linda Korotkich (13)
St David's High School, Dalkeith

THE FINAL

In the dressing rooms we're waiting for the squad to be named.
Come on lads it's our turn, we can win this game.
The ref came in and says the game's about to start.
Right lads time to play with all your heart.
Whoee the whistle blew,
Whoom the chosen players flew.
I got the ball and ran to the goals,
I was in the box, the keeper was off his line.
I was sure I could score, the goal was mine.
I took the shot,
I scored: I screamed and everybody cheered and jumped.
I looked round at the keeper, he was getting thumped.
The whistle went, it was the end of the game.
Everybody ran towards me, I was enjoying my moment of fame.
We went over to get our cup and medal,
Everyone was pleased,
But I was cheesed.
I felt like I had won the World Cup not just the League Cup,
But all the great players have to start somewhere.

Steven Nethery (13)
St David's High School, Dalkeith

THE THING

What is that? I don't know.
Is it something you can
See like TV or the sky?

Or is it something you
Can smell like a rose
Or oil?

Is it something you
Can hear like water
In a river?

Or is it something you
Can touch like snow
Or rain?

I know - it is a poem.

Jacqueline Wilson (12)
St David's High School, Dalkeith

HORSES

Horses, horses, galloping around,
Galloping wild, galloping free,
Galloping through water, galloping through fields,
Galloping all day, such fit and wild creatures.

Horses, horses, lots of horses,
Different shapes, different sizes,
Different lengths, different heights,
Different natures, such beautiful creatures.

Horses, horses, animals that need love,
Animals that need attention,
Animals that need work,
Animals that need a home,
Such demanding creatures.

Horses, horses, many different breeds,
The miniature Shetland, the gigantic Clydesdale.

Ruaraidh Szanel (13)
St David's High School, Dalkeith

THE RAIN

The drop, it's fallen,
It's getting closer, closer
And *crash*.

It soaked me on the
Head with a splash,
Then after more fell,
Down one by one,
Down, down, and
Then *splash*.

I am soaking to the
Skin, I am *soaking wet*.

The puddle goes splosh,
Worse, I stand in the puddle,
It wets my feet, it
Makes a splash, the feeling is
Gooey and wet. I am
Going to dry my feet off
In a nice warm, cosy house.
Cheerio, goodnight, I am *dry*.

Naomi Cameron (13)
St David's High School, Dalkeith

SNOWDROPS

In the far away distance you see it fall,
The tiny little thing that amazes all.
It comes from the north and ends in the west
The lovely little thing that I love best,
        Snowdrops.

People playing in the snow making angels and who else knows,
It starts as a small bit, tiny as rain,
And ends in an avalanche that will scare yi home.

After the avalanche, people come out,
Crunch, crunch walking about.
When you're out there in the snow,
There's kids running about in places I don't go.

The day goes quick from day to night,
And the kids go in and all say goodnight.

Craig Glen (12)
St David's High School, Dalkeith

DISCO

Discos are amazing
With all the flashing lights,
Everyone is dancing all through the night.
People jumping up and down,
Look at them just go,
But in the morning when they get up
They're walking really slow.

Lindsey Traynor (13)
St David's High School, Dalkeith

WORLD WAR II

Roughed and scuffed bombshells lie
On the bloodstained poppy fields.
Soldiers scream out in pain as
Miniature pieces of steel pierce their legs.
All this pain and suffering - what for?

Men run from the trenches hoping
They will come back.
If they don't they will only be
One added to the thousands and
Thousands killed on this battlefield.

Far off in the distance they can
Hear the gentle threatening groan
Coming from the engines of the
German airforce.

In the darkness of night at some early
Hour the air raid siren starts screaming
Like someone has grabbed a cat by
The tail and is swinging it around.
Suddenly panic breaks out around the
Camp, men are running half dressed, screaming,
Searching for their guns.

At the end of it the world is silent,
All is silent, silent with sadness.

Steven Colston (12)
St David's High School, Dalkeith

HARLEY DAVIDSON

H ear the power,
A ll the silver and gold,
R evving up the engine,
L eaning on the turns,
E ngine is 1350cc,
Y ou have to be careful.

D angerous we know,
A ll the leathers,
V reg of course,
I 've never been on one,
D o 205 in 5 gears,
S o, so fast,
O n the seat, hot with leather,
N ever seen one pass me, far too fast.

Alan Meikle (13)
St David's High School, Dalkeith

THE SEA

The sea is cold,
The sea is hot, the waves come in,
They go back out,
And when they do they take some shells.
The seaweed's green, it feels so slimy,
They wobble about and feel horrible.
I wonder if at the bottom it's dark
Or if it's light and if it's dark would
Fish live there or would there be any?

Craig McKenzie (12)
St David's High School, Dalkeith

TRAMPOLINING

Bouncing, jumping,
Twirling and flipping.

Upside down,
Over and under.

Up and down,
Round and round.

Front drops,
Back drops,
Seat drops.

The moves much harder
Than they look.

Tuck jump,
Straddle jump,
Pike jump.

These are easier
Than most of them.

Front somersault,
Back somersault,
Pike fronts.

These can break
Your legs.

So when you're trampolining
Be very *careful!*

Louise Severn (13)
St David's High School, Dalkeith

I Should Like To . . .

I should like to touch the glow of the stars in the universe,
Feel the breeze of a comet passing through space.
I should like to feel the joy of an athlete
After trying and winning their very first race.

I should like to be in the minds of the gods:
What did they feel when Jesus was born?
I should like to console the victims of war
After the death of their friends and family they mourn.

I should like to touch the happiness of a mother
After giving birth to her very first child.
I should like to help an animal in captivity
To gain freedom and go back to the wild.

I should like to paint the fear of an army in battle,
Talk to those who are in heaven without being dead.
I should like to know the joy and experience
Of being able to paint the White House red.

I should like to dive into the depths of the ocean,
Ride on a sea horse all day and all night.
I should like to experience an average thing
Like going to the park and flying my kite.

I should like to paint what Disney felt
The day Snow White was shown.
I should like to touch the happiness of a child
After eating their chocolate ice-cream cone.

I should like to do and see many things,
Here I mention only a few.
I should like to live a very full life,
And every day try something new.

Shereen Peshrowian (13)
St Margaret's & St Denis & Cranley School

THE LOST FOREST

Outlined against the undying sky
It towered.
A Goliath creature
Untamed and wild
With jagged teeth and harsh glaring eyes.
It moved, chopping its way towards us,
Demolishing anything and everything.
Closer and closer it came until,
It was almost upon us.
We cowered away and tried to run
But we were rooted to the spot.
And then,
It was there, upon us,
You humans felled us all.

Arwen Buchanan (14)
Trinity Academy

BETRAYAL

As she lay there wounded a tear drops from my eye,
Nothing is said but a soft silent sigh.
Was it today that her life was to come to an end?
She was all I had to live for much more than a friend.
The feeling of sickness fills my mind,
Happiness in the future I will not find.
In my blood covered hand I lay down the gun,
The feeling of guilt sweeps through me as I now realise what I've done.
Why did I do it? I don't know, but for what she did, she had to go.

Gail Sangster (12)
Trinity Academy

BROKEN MEMORIES

You've forgotten -
  haven't you?

You've forgotten the music,
You've forgotten the chatting and the laughter,
You've forgotten the fun, the dancing, the twirling skirts,
The white wine, and the single red rose -
  haven't you?

You've forgotten the smiles,
You've forgotten the warmth and the happiness,
You've forgotten the joy, the romance, the glistening jewels,
The open skies, and the starry kiss -
  haven't you?

You've forgotten your promise,
You've forgotten your hasty, misleading promise,
You've forgotten what you said when the end came too soon,
And you promised you'd never forget me -
  haven't you?

Morag Brown (14)
Trinity Academy

SCHOOL

School is a place
Where we all have to go.
Getting told things
We don't want to know.
Where teachers scream
And pupils shout.
And life can be ruled
By a bullying lout.

Robert Abbott (12)
Whitburn Academy

WHY ME?

Why me?
Am I so different from you?
I watched Red Dwarf last night
I thought it was funny,
I heard you did too.

Why me?
Am I so different from you?
I was home late yesterday,
I got grounded,
I heard you did too.

Why me?
Am I so different from you?
I have a vast collection of
World Wrestling Federation videos,
I heard you collect them too.

Why me?
Am I so different from you?
Why do you bully me?
Am I not a human being
Too?

Scott Bigham (12)
Whitburn Academy

I'VE GOT THE FLU!

I've got sweat running like a hose,
With a bit of a chill.
I have a blocked nose
'Cause I'm very ill.

Covers up to my chin,
Lying on the leather couch,
My head has its own heart
Thumping like a drum. Ouch!

Here comes the doctor
In his little yellow Mini.
He was wearing baggy clothes
But he was awful skinny.

He shoved a thermometer in my mouth
And a stethoscope on my chest.
He held my wrist and counted to ten,
Then said, 'It's the flu, just get some rest.'

Mum gave me a glass of water,
And put a cloth on my head.
She gave me two Paracetamols
Then sent me off to bed.

I cuddled into my teddy
And tried to get some sleep,
But I was up half the night coughing
So I started counting sheep.

It's great to be off school so long,
But the flu part is driving me mad.
I'll be glad when all this is over
Then I can stop being sad.

To school I would rather go
Than be home with the flu you know.

Claire Cuthbert (13)
Whitburn Academy

LIFE

Life is for you to live not
To waste away, so go out
And have some fun and try
And make your day.

Live life to the full, that's what people
Say, so why not make
The most of each and every day?

Days can be happy but
Days can be sad so take
Life as it comes and
Capture it in your hands.

Life should be good
From the day that you
Are born and even when
You wake up each and
Every morn.

But if someone dies don't hold
Back, your life, just keeps on going
And you'll be alright.

Sarah Penman (13)
Whitburn Academy

THE CIRCUS

The circus is coming,
The circus is here,
Clowns dancing so very near.

The smell of the greasepaint,
The roar of the crowd,
Dancing, singing, music so loud.

The lions and tigers are all there,
Excitement and laughter everywhere,
Acrobats leaping in the air.

And so it's all over,
The lights all go out,
The circus is great, we all roar and shout!

Kirstie Paton (11)
Whitburn Academy

WAR

Whenever I open a newspaper
Or turn on the news
All I see is war.
Wars causing tears,
Wars causing pain,
Wars causing anger,
Wars causing fears,
Wars causing hatred,
Wars causing death.
I think to myself
Why does this happen?
But I can't think of any reason except
Selfishness, greed and the need to destroy.

Sandra Dundas (12)
Whitburn Academy

FRIEND

When I need her, guess who is there?
    Mum, to cheer me up again!

When I am sad, guess who makes me happy?
    Mum, for when my dad left me!

When I am sick, guess who makes me well?
    Mum, by telling me what gossip I have missed!

When I am hurt, guess who picks me up?
    Mum, when I came tumbling off my horse!

When I need a friend, guess who is always there?
    Mum, my best friend.

Holly Allan (12)
Whitburn Academy

FEAR

It lives but it never dies,
You scream but you never know why.
A ghostly figure flies by,
Never trust something that you can't see.

Is your worst fear to be murdered?
A murderer could stalk you or scare you to death,
Carving you up like meat in a butcher's shop,
Might be fun to be a psycho.

Spiders are definitely the queen of all fears.

Vikki Boyd (13)
Whitburn Academy

The Countdown

There's been a big fuss about the
millennium for months now, and all it is,
is just another boring year.
What is the fuss about?
I certainly don't know. Do you?
But what will happen on January 1st 2000?
Will we all starve because the machines
have broken down?
Will the streets be in chaos with people
breaking in to every house in sight?
Will rich become poor?
Will all ends of the world join together for
the fight for survival?
Or will we turn against each other, friends
becoming enemies, fighting for survival alone?
Who knows?

Stephanie Gardiner (12)
Whitburn Academy

Football Is The Greatest

F   ootball is the greatest
O   f all our national sports
O   utdoors in most weathers
T   raining to be the best
B   est wins all the trophies
A   dmiration from all the fans
L   oving every minute
L   onging for the next game.

William Cook (13)
Whitburn Academy

COLOURS

Red is the colour of love,
which is the colour for passion.

Yellow is the colour of the sun,
shining in the sky.

Pink is the colour of roses,
blossoming in spring.

Green is the colour of trees,
swaying in the wind.

Orange is the colour of a tiger,
roaring in the jungle.

Purple is the colour of tulips
which are found in Holland.

Blue is the colour of the sea,
splashing in the wind.

Put all these colours together
and you will get a rainbow.

Sharon Watson (13)
Whitburn Academy

WOULD YOU?

If there was no peace would you accept war?
If there was no justice would you accept crime?
If there was no leadership would you accept chaos?
If there was no money would you accept poverty?
If there was no life would you accept death?
If you could change the world, would you?

John Hamilton (12)
Whitburn Academy

SARAH

As I'm looking round the classroom
I turn to my left and there she is,
With her long brown hair
She lets it straggle with no care,
Laughing with her friends
With not a touch of fear in her head.
When she begins to work
Her hand moves and does not stop,
Her lovely creamy skin
Stands out in the crowd,
Her blue eyes screaming out so loud
And she is very proud of all her work.
And she really likes having fun,
Joking around
With her special ones
And that is my friend, Sarah.

Charlene Clark (12)
Whitburn Academy

I HAVE A DREAM

I have a dream,
a dream to become a football superstar,
to play for Scotland in the World Cup,
to hear the crowd cheer my name,
to be the best striker in the world,
to be greater than the football greats,
then one day become manager of a team,
to make my team the best team in the world,
to make all the players want to play for my team.
That's my dream.

Eddie Lennon (12)
Whitburn Academy

NATURE

The tiger that roars,
The fish that soars,
The rain that pours,
Are all part of nature.

> The rivers that flow,
> The wind that blows,
> The snail, so slow,
> Are all part of nature!

The sun that shines,
The trees of pine,
The spider's web so fine,
Are all part of nature.

Lindsay Smith (12)
Whitburn Academy

OH BROTHER

O   nly little sisters know,
H   ow big brothers can bug them so.

B   ut though we love them,
R   ascals they always are.
O   ddness comes in there too,
T   hen we fight and have arguments.
H   is messiness makes me tidy.
E   very day he annoys me.
R   eally I love him. Shush!

Yvonne Harper (12)
Whitburn Academy

SECOND WORLD WAR

The year was 1939
The war had just begun,
Britain Vs Germany
Oh what a terrible one.
Winston Churchill went to battle,
He was a fearless man,
He was brave and strong,
He won the hearts of many.
The year was now 1945,
Britain had won the war,
There were parties and balls,
Oh how happy they were.
Germany was happy too,
There was no killing any more.

Cameron Macintyre (12)
Whitburn Academy

MY DREAM

One day I'd like to drive a truck,
Be it Volvo, Scania or Merc.
For Eddie Stobart I'd like to work,
The biggest company in Europe,
Down the motorway I shall fly
With my jacket and my tie,
With over nine hundred lorries on the road
I will carry a very heavy load,
But as I am only thirteen
All of this is just a dream.

Barrie Paterson (13)
Whitburn Academy

WHEN THE CLOCK STRIKES TWELVE

On the 31st of December
When the big mahogany clock strikes
Twelve,
We'll all jump, sing and shout,
Well have a happy new year,
But some of us
Will think of the year 2000,
We'll wonder if the world will end,
Or if there will be a difference.
But what I think of the year 2000,
You just won't care,
For it's only another year.
But we'll find out all about the year 2000
When the big mahogany clock strikes
Twelve.

Jennifer Moonie (13)
Whitburn Academy

MY LITTLE BROTHER

Joe Joe is his nickname,
Playing football is his game,
To be a Celtic player is his aim.

His hair, blond as ever,
Eating, that's something he never does,
But playing football, that's something he loves.
Coming home to his big, bright smile
Is the highlight of my day.
I can't stand it when he has to go away.
I have just described my little brother for you.
Oh, and by the way, his name is Jordan.

Ashleigh McNeill (12)
Whitburn Academy

WEATHER

Weather, weather everywhere,
Weather's made up in the air.
Rain and sun, wind and snow,
Weather makes you glow,
Not always!

Weather, weather can be good,
Weather, weather can be bad.
When the weather's bad
It makes people really sad,
Not always!

Weather, weather can be bad,
But it can make people very glad.
Kids and toddlers play in it.
Weather, weather's the greatest bit.

Graham Bell (12)
Whitburn Academy

GLITTER

Glitter, glitter everywhere,
Glitter, glitter in my hair,
Glitter, glitter all sparkly,
Wear it when you go to a party.

You can get red, you can get blue,
You can get any colour it's up to you,
Let it be bold, let it be flash,
All you need is the *cash*.

Amanda-Jo Hendry (12)
Whitburn Academy

MY THREE CATS

She was cute, she was big,
She was my first cat.
Cute and fat
She lay all day sleeping,
And also always eating.
Playing when she can be bothered,
Lazily lying as she's now exhausted,
That's my cat, Jess.

She roamed the streets cold and lost,
She sneaked in once and slept all day,
She was a stray.
We put up notes but no replies,
She stayed and stayed,
She was a little rat
Running under our feet,
Prancing up and down the street
That was my cat, Mog.

He found our home one day,
We knew he was a stray,
He stayed for a week or so.
When I was down the street
I met some friends,
Her son was missing a cat.
Playing all the time,
Eating and sleeping is his best.
Today he plays and stays
That's my cat, Boy.

Ami Dempster (12)
Whitburn Academy

THE HUNTING TIGER

He crouches low in the yellow grass
Sizing up the wildebeest's mass.
Then he moves in for the kill,
Hunting is the tiger's thrill.

There is no strength a tiger lacks,
A poor wildebeest he attacks.
The creature, not knowing its fate
Realises when it's too late.

At last the tiger will get a good meal,
Finally his hunger will heal.
His hunting skills are extremely good
But soon he will be craving food!

Leigh Heron (12)
Whitburn Academy

BEANIES

Millennium is the prettiest
with the gold bow,
Her friend has big angel wings,
her name is Halo.

Goochy is colourful, the most
ticklish jellyfish you'll ever meet,
Even though he is cute
he has no feet.

Scat is the cat with the grey coat
and pink nose,
Max tries hard to prove he's the best
swinging his bat harder than the rest.

Stacey Dunn (12)
Whitburn Academy

WINDOW OF THE WORLD

I look out of the window
and what do I see?
Everyone living together in
perfect harmony.

Of course this is just a dream because
when I look out of the window,
what do I see?
Fighting and killing,
sadness and misery.

Wars are raging,
people are dying,
bombs exploding,
the world crying!

In this life we have to work together!

So whether a boy in Kosovo,
or a girl in Taiwan,
can't we just work together
following God's plan?

Because

In the future when I look out of the window
I want to see
everyone living together
in perfect harmony.

This is my dream!

Gemma Lundie (13)
Whitburn Academy

Loneliness Through Life

Loneliness,
It happens when you're going on your way,
It spots you and it reckons
You'll be easy prey.
You won't fight your inner demons,
It's time you learned to pray
Because once they take you prisoner
They'll make you play their games!

Loneliness is with you through the day and the night,
A predator it stalks you, relentless in its plight,
Slowly as you waken it makes you shiver with fright,
It's gripping onto you with all its might!

Oh loneliness,
It's with you
As you travel along your way,
A never-ending demon
Having fun at play,
It messes with your head,
And when you lay down on the floor
It haunts you
In your dreams,
Saying you'll be alone forever more!

Loneliness will take you as unsuspecting prey,
It will make you want to be alone
All through night and day,
So don't you listen to that voice
As it echoes in your head,
If you do you might as well be dead,
Because loneliness it kills you,
Your heart and your soul!

Loneliness it stops
The things you say
And do,
So it's up to you,
You must be brave
And true!

But most of all
Be you!

Lianne Jones (12)
Whitburn Academy

CHRISTMAS

C   hristmas time is full of glee
H   appy children putting up their tree
R   udolph getting prepared for his journey
I   cy snow gleaming like pearls
S   now falling silently, slowly to the ground
T   he feeling of joy in the air
M   istletoe above everyone's door
A   nd a gleaming present under every tree
S   anta checking who has been good or bad.
T   insel glittering and a star on the tree
I   cicles so clear hanging from the roof
M   um in the kitchen cooking the crispy chicken
E   veryone, it's *Christmas Day.*

Christmastime is full of joy
With the pretty, crispy chicken,
Silent snow and the tinselled tree.
All these things make Christmas Day
Such a merry, happy day.

Zoe Livingstone (11)
Whitburn Academy

SPACE, STAR WARS

S pace, the emptiness,
P luto, Mars, these are some of the planets,
A final frontier for mankind.
C alling all aliens, is there anyone out there?
E asy to reach with these new rockets.

S tarships, lasers, new races of aliens,
T ogether they fight against the Empire,
A nakin Skywalker, Darth Vader,
R aging in battle, Luke and Darth.

W eb-footed aliens and humped-back aliens,
A lways in battle, light sabres clashing,
R ifles firing on Tatooine,
S tar Wars - it never ends.

Colin Simpson (12)
Whitburn Academy

MY FRIENDS

My friends are cool,
My friends are smart,
They're the best in the school.

First there's Sharon who's a klutz,
Second there's Elana who's bonkers, just a touch,
Third there's Laura who worries about the time,
Fourth there's Zoe who's thick as a pine,
Then there's Lindsay who's just football mad.

My friends are the best,
Plus they're much better than the rest.

Natalie Myron (12)
Whitburn Academy

MY SECRET PLACE!

I have a very secret place,
Where I can travel through outer space,
I can pay a visit to the queen
Many places I have seen.

I can roll in flowers under a tree,
In my place I feel totally free,
There are always rainbows in the sky,
But they disappear and I don't know why.

I meet many people in my place,
I know each and every face,
Everyone there is my friend,
But sooner or later it comes to an end.

I enjoy the rainbows and the trees,
The people there that care for me,
I enjoy the glow of the golden sun,
I like the place where I skip and run.

The special place isn't just for me,
Your imagination is the key.
Places like mine are a lot of fun
And they're free to each and everyone!

If you're feeling sad or feeling blue,
Escape to the place that's made for you,
Only you have the key,
So take my advice and think like me!

Gillian Pearson (12)
Whitburn Academy

School Day

I wake up to drag myself out of my bed,
It is like pulling an elephant near a mouse, impossible!
The thorny bushes of my hair are so noticeable,
I put on my 'designer' uniform and take my
'rabbit food' lunch to the front door.
I start to walk down the road that leads to the prison
which is our school.
The roads today are empty,
No parents looking in a panic for a parking space
to drop their children off.
But as I turn into the gate where we usually
see the smiling faces,
there are no cars or teachers to be seen,
all there seems to be is an unsettling silence.
I then remember to my horror, it is Saturday!

Lisa Webster (12)
Whitburn Academy

I Have A Dream

I have a dream
For Rangers to reign supreme,
Conquer Scotland,
Conquer Europe,
Conquer the world,
To beat the rest
And beat the best,
To be the best team,
That is my dream.

Robert Stewart (12)
Whitburn Academy

A POEM

I need to write a poem,
but I don't know what about.
'Anything you want,' I'm told,
but I still can't decide.

It hangs over your head:
whether to make it rhyme or not;
whether to illustrate it,
or to leave it blank.

It's hard to decide the background,
or the style to do it in,
but as I've found out,
poems are really hard to write.

Beverley Sutherland (12)
Whitburn Academy

A MAN'S BEST FRIEND

As the seasons change, one thing will always be the same,
The greeting from my best friend.
Come rain or shine, night or day, she will always treat me the same.
Four legs, a tail and fur, she's always there for me,
She is faithful, smart and obedient, she's also very quick,
She knows what time I come home,
I think she tries to talk.
When I am lonely or sad, she makes me feel happy.
If I'm bored, I play with her.
I wouldn't be very happy if she wasn't there for me.

Robert Watson (13)
Whitburn Academy

TATTIES

Tatties in a pot,
Tatties nice and hot,
Tatties that I eat,
Nice and sweet.

Tatties with butter,
Tatties in a clutter,
Tatties whole,
Tatties in a bowl.

Tatties boiled,
Tatties baked,
Just eat your tatties,
For goodness sake.

Don't get suspicious,
They're just delicious,
They are gid,
But they're just fid!

Tatties in a pot,
Tatties nice and hot,
Tatties that I eat,
Nice and sweet.

Stacey Watson (13)
Whitburn Academy

MY BEANIES

Millennium the bear, is bright pink.
She's the specialist I'd make you think.
This one has a nice gold bow,
The real millennium will come and go.

Princess is purple with a white rose,
With black eyes and a little brown nose.
She has a white bow,
She was named after the princess we all know.

Fortune the panda is black and white,
From a dream or a childhood delight.
With her nice name she wants you to know
When she's around, your luck will never be low.

Prickles the hedgehog is so loveable and cute,
She is not even the size of your foot!
With her black nose and little eyes,
At the end of the busy night she sighs.

These are a few of my favourite beanies here
I fear nothing while they are with me, so
Don't shed a tear.

Teri Overend (12)
Whitburn Academy